Longman GARDENER'S DICTIONARY

Emma Dally and
Catherine Carpenter

Longman Group UK Limited,
Longman House, Burnt Mill, Harlow,
Essex CM20 2JE, England
and Associated Companies throughout the world.

First published 1986

British Library Cataloguing in Publication Data

Longman gardener's dictionary
1. Gardening — Dictionaries
635′.03′21 SB450.95

ISBN 0 582 89248 1

Printed in Great Britain
by Mackays Ltd, Chatham, Kent

Illustrations by Jerry Collins

About the authors

Emma Dally, a keen and experienced gardener, is literary editor of *Cosmopolitan*. Catherine Carpenter works freelance and has edited several books on gardening.

Contents

Abbreviations used in the dictionary

abb	abbreviation
adj	adjective
n	noun
pl	plural
vi	intransitive verb
vt	transitive verb

Illustrations

Introduction

GARDENING is one of the most popular hobbies in this country, cutting across all barriers to be enjoyed by men and women, young and old, rich and poor. The size of the gardener's patch is not important; all gardens need to be planned, maintained, fed and loved, and the tiniest plot of cultivated land can generate as much fascination and enthusiasm in the person who tends it as a large and well stocked estate.

An interest in gardening can develop at any age but it usually appears when one gets one's first garden. This may be established and needing maintenance, or neglected and needing inspiring plans to make it perfect, or even just a bare patch of earth churned up by builders. It may be only a few square feet or half an acre; it may be a container garden on the roof or it may be an allotment half a mile from the home. Whatever the size and shape of the garden, the potential is there to make plants grow, flower, fruit and flourish. Much of the new gardener's early excitement comes from the realization of a vast new world opening up. There is so much to learn about it all – plants, the soil, growing conditions, propagation – and plenty of time to take it all in and experiment. But first the language of gardening has to be learned.

Like most activities, gardening has its own language, or jargon, which gardeners use when they talk to each other about their plants and gardens, giving advice, swapping cuttings and sharing seedlings. Most of it is very specific and useful, but to the novice it can be incomprehensible. And because it is a language peculiar to gardening, many of the terms cannot be found in a general dictionary.

Although newspaper gardening columns are invaluable sources of information for the amateur gardener, they are all written by experts who sometimes forget that not everyone will be familiar with the words they use. Many gardening books, excellent in every other way, are guilty of speaking only to the initiated.

This dictionary is aimed chiefly at new gardeners who want to understand the basic terms used in gardening columns and books while they tackle their first patch of land – although we hope too that even experienced gardeners may find some unfamiliar information in it. We have tried to provide information about every aspect of gardening except the individual plants themselves: gardening operations and techniques, the tools, equipment, foods and chemicals that are used, the main pests and diseases that are encountered, the terms used to describe various plants and plant-parts.

This book should be used as a companion when reading or hearing about gardening and will allow newcomers to communicate properly with any one of the millions of others who share an enthusiasm for the most relaxing, creative and ancient of pastimes.

Emma Dally
Catherine Carpenter

abscission n
the natural separation of flowers, fruit or leaves from a plant at a special separation layer, eg, the shedding of leaves from a deciduous tree in autumn.

acaricide n
any inorganic dust or spray used to control MITES.

acaulescent adj
(of a flower) having or appearing to have no stem.

accelerator n
any of various fertilizers that are added to compost in order to hasten rotting. Also known as an activator.

accent plant n
a plant which by its shape or colouring provides a contrast with surrounding plants or serves to emphasize a feature of garden design.

acclimatize vt
to cause (a plant) to adapt to conditions different from those in which it has grown previously. See also HARDEN OFF.

achene, akene n
a small dry one-seeded fruit (eg of the dandelion or buttercup) that does not split open at maturity.

acicular adj
(of a leaf) shaped like a needle.
acid adj
(of soil) having no free lime and a PH content of less than 6.5. Plants that are CALCIFUGES hate lime and therefore thrive in acid soil, but to grow other plants in the same soil it may be necessary to add lime. The acid quality of soil may affect the appearance of plants grown in it; eg the flowers of certain hydrangeas grown in acid soil are blue, while those grown in ALKALINE soil are pink.
acid-loving plant n
see CALCIFUGE.
acorn n
the fruit of the oak tree, usually seated in or surrounded by a hard woody cup (CUPULE).
actinomorphic, actinomorphous adj
(of a flower) capable of being divided symmetrically by more than one plane passing lengthwise through the central axis, eg the rose. Compare ZYGOMORPHIC.
activator n
see ACCELERATOR.
active-growth period n
the time of year in which a plant produces new growth in the form of shoots, leaves and usually flowers. During this time plants require more feeding and watering than they do in the dormant period when they are not growing.
acuminate adj
(of a plant organ) tapering to a slender point.

acute adj
(of a leaf or petal) terminating in a sharp point.
adelgid n
a sap-sucking insect related to the aphid. Adelgids mainly infest conifers and can be controlled by spring spraying with MALATHION, DERRIS or SYSTEMIC insecticides.
adpressed, appressed adj
(of a plant organ) close to or lying flat against another organ of the same plant.
adult adj
(of plant growth or foliage) having a leaf shape distinctly different from that of the JUVENILE foliage. The eucalyptus is one tree with such foliage.
adventitious adj
(of a root or shoot) arising from an unexpected position. Usually a result of cutting back the stem or root of a plant, an adventitious shoot may grow from the stump even though no DORMANT bud was present.
aerate vt
to supply (soil) with an adequate amount of air for healthy growing conditions. This is usually done by digging, forking and hoeing, and adding organic matter to the soil. A lawn is aerated by pricking with a fork or an AERATOR.
aerator n
a tool with a spiked roller used to aerate the surface of a lawn.
aerial bud n
a bud that exists or grows from part of a plant in

the air rather than in the ground.

aerial root n

a root that grows from the stem of a plant above ground and does not usually root into the soil. Such roots absorb moisture from the atmosphere and provide support for certain plants, eg ivy and Virginia creeper.

air frost n

a freezing temperature measured with a thermometer in a slatted container 4 ft (1.2 m) above the grass surface. See also GROUND FROST.

air layering n

a method of propagating a plant by inducing the formation of roots on branches or shoots that are attached to the parent plant but are too high or stiff to be layered at soil level. The stem is wounded immediately beneath a joint and the wound is dusted with hormone rooting powder. Damp SPHAGNUM MOSS is tied in and around it, and covered with polythene. Roots appear through the moss after a few weeks. This method is often used with tall houseplants, eg the rubber plant. Also known as Chinese layering, marcottage and pot-layering.

aldrin n

a chlorinated insecticide used mainly for the control of soil pests such as WIREWORMS and LEATHER JACKETS. Aldrin is highly toxic to human beings.

algae n pl

microscopic plants that form a green scum in

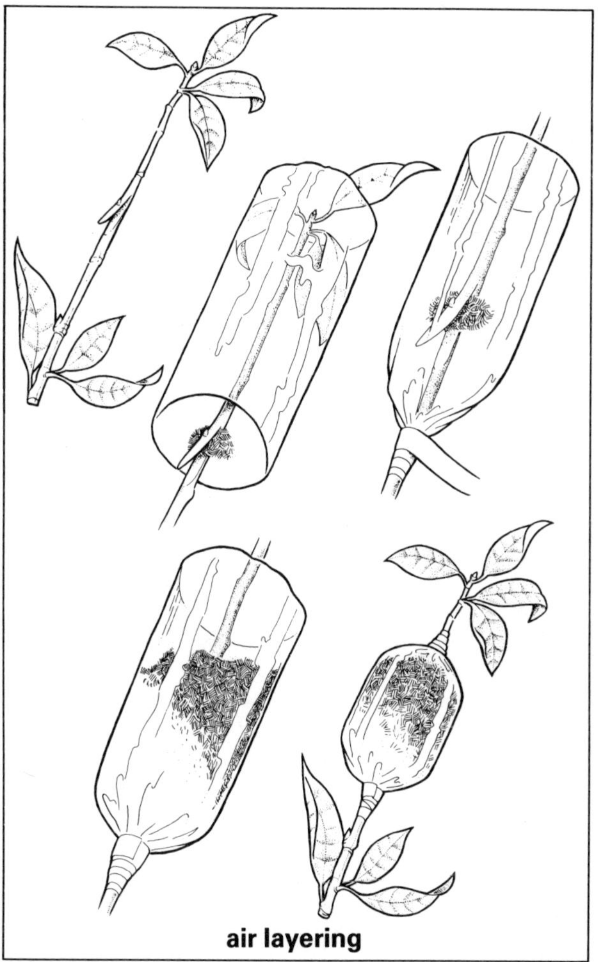

air layering

stagnant water and on damp surfaces. Certain pond algae, such as blanketweed or silkweed, can grow rapidly and restrict the growth of other plants. They can be removed by hand or with a net. Algae can be killed with chemicals, eg SULPHATE OF COPPER, but care must be taken to follow the manufacturer's instructions to avoid serious damage to other plants.

algicide n

any of various substances that kill algae. Algicides usually contain chemicals such as SULPHATE OF COPPER and potassium permanganate. Alginex, for example, is a powerful preparation for use on paths, walls and flowerpots and is used heavily diluted with water.

alginate n

an INORGANIC soil conditioner derived from SEAWEED. It is used to bind the finer particles in heavy soil to produce a more manageable texture.

alkaline adj

(of soil) having a PH of more than 7.3. Soils that contain a great deal of LIME or CHALK are usually alkaline. They are excellent for CALCICOLES but are not suitable for CALCIFUGES. Alkaline soil is often described as chalky or limy.

allotment n

a small plot of land, one of many into which a larger piece of land is divided, that is let out to individuals by a council for cultivation. Allotments in Britain are generally used for growing vegetables and fruits; in some areas, by-laws may restrict the growing of ornamental plants. They are a useful amenity for people without a sizable garden.

alpine n

a plant native to the Alps or northern parts of the northern hemisphere, eg *Dianthus alpinus* and *Leontopodium* (Edelweiss). Broadly, any of various small plants suitable for growing in a ROCK GARDEN or ALPINE HOUSE, eg smaller gentians and primulas.

alpine house n

an unheated, well-ventilated greenhouse designed for the growing of alpines or other rock plants which will not winter satisfactorily in the open, or are seen to better advantage when protected from wind, rain and frost.

alternate adj

(of plant parts) arranged singly first on one side and then on the other at different heights or points along a stem, flower stalk etc. Compare OPPOSITE.

ammonium sulphamate n

a powerful weedkiller. Often given in the abbreviation AMS, this should not be confused with SULPHATE OF AMMONIA, which is fertilizer. Land treated with AMS should not be planted with food crops for 12 weeks. It may also damage roots of nearby trees.

amplexicaul adj

(of a leaf) having no stalk and a base that surrounds the plant stem. Leaves of this type, eg

in *Doronicum* (Leopard's bane), are sometimes referred to as clasping.

androecium n

all the STAMENS in the flower of a SEED PLANT, viewed collectively.

anemone-centred adj

(*of a composite flower*) having central TUBULAR FLORETS which form a cushion shape, sometimes of a different colour, among the flat RAY FLORETS. This term is often applied to chrysanthemums and dahlias.

angiosperm n

any of the class (*Angiospermae*) of SEED PLANTS having their seeds in a closed OVARY. Among the better-known angiosperms are buttercups, orchids, roses, oaks and grasses. They are also known as flowering plants. Compare GYMNOSPERM.

[1]**annual** n

1 a plant that grows from seed, flowers and dies in one growing season. Annuals are divided into HARDY, HALF-HARDY and TENDER depending on their resistance to adverse weather conditions. **2** Loosely, any PERENNIAL which can grow from seed and flower in one growing season, eg antirrhinum. Also known as a bedding perennial.

[2]**annual** adj

(*of a plant*) growing from seed, flowering and dying in one growing season.

annulation n

the disappearance of DORMANT buds on a plant stem or branch after a period of years. This may be avoided in fruit trees by careful pruning, which stimulates the growth of such buds.

ant n

any of a family of insects, related to the bees and wasps, that live in large colonies. Ants can be a pest in the garden: they may undermine plants when building a nest; they protect several other pests, such as aphids and mealy bugs; they may steal seeds, especially those of brassicas; and red ants can inflict a painful sting. On the other hand, they feed on such pests as caterpillars and wireworms, and their excavations may help to aerate the soil. Severe infestations can be controlled by various pesticides.

anterior adj

(of a plant part) facing away from the stem or axis.

anther n

the part of a STAMEN that contains and releases POLLEN. It is usually ovoid in shape and comprises two pollen sacs joined on a stalk.

anthracnose n

any of various plant diseases caused by a FUNGUS and characterized by the appearance of dark sunken spots or blisters.

anti-transpirant n

a substance sprayed on leaves to inhibit TRANSPIRATION and thus lessen the plant's water loss. This is particularly useful when transplanting evergreens in full leaf, as at this time their roots may not be able to take up enough water. Also called transplanting spray.

apetalous adj
(of a flower) having no petals.
apex n, pl **apexes, apices**
the tip of a shoot or branch.
aphid n
any of a related group of small insects that suck the juices from the stems and leaves of plants. These include the well-known GREENFLY and BLACKFLY. They do much damage in the garden, checking plant growth, causing leaf curl and discoloration, and seriously reducing the quality and quantity of the floral display. They are most damaging, however, as virus carriers, transferring disease from infected to healthy plants. Aphids reproduce at a rapid rate and should be destroyed as soon as they appear. They can be controlled with any insecticide containing MALATHION, DERRIS, HCH or NICOTINE. SYSTEMIC insecticides containing MENAZON can also be used. During the winter, aphid eggs can be destroyed with a TAR OIL WASH.
apical adj
(*of a shoot*) situated at or forming the apex of a plant.
apiculate adj
(of a leaf) ending abruptly in a small point.
apogamy n
the development of a plant embryo from a female reproductive cell without fertilization, eg in some ferns.
apomixis n, pl **apomixes**
reproduction (eg APOGAMY and

PARTHENOGENESIS) involving the production of seed without fertilization.

approach graft n

a type of graft in which the SCION is left attached to the parent ROOTSTOCK and growing on its own roots until it is united with the second rootstock. The plants supplying rootstock and scion must be growing close together, usually in separate pots. The tissues of each plant are partially cut and the cut surfaces bound together until they unite. If the plant supplying the scion cannot be brought close to the rootstock, a BOTTLE GRAFT is used. An approach graft is often used to propagate vines. Also known as inarch. Also **approach-graft** vt.

aquatic adj

(of a plant) growing in water. There are three groups of aquatic plants: those that have their leaves and flowers above water and their roots submerged (eg water lily); those that are entirely floating (eg duckweed); and those that are wholly submerged except for their flowers (eg water violets). See also MARGINAL and OXYGENATOR.

arachnoid adj

(of a plant part) covered with or composed of soft loose hairs or fibres.

arboretum n

a place where trees and shrubs are cultivated for study and display.

arbour n

a shady retreat protected by trees or climbing

plants grown over trelliswork.

arcillite n

an absorbent granular material, made from a clayey mineral which has been crushed, dried and baked, that can be used as an ingredient in composts, a soil conditioner or a topdressing for lawns. Compare PERLITE and VERMICULITE.

arcure n

a decorative method of training fruit trees, eg apple or pear, so that their branches grow in bow-shaped arches. The branches are trained first one way, then the other way. New shoots grow from one DORMANT bud; the other buds are pruned to form fruiting SPURS.

areole n

a modified side shoot on some members of the CACTUS family, resembling a small pincushion which bears flowers, woolly or barbed hairs and new shoots.

aristate adj

(of a plant part) having AWNS.

armed adj

(of a plant) having spines, thorns or prickles.

aroid n

a plant from the *Araceae* family, eg the arum lily or the flamingo flower, which is characterized by an INFLORESCENCE comprised of an erect SPADIX with masses of tiny flowers and a single SPATHE of an impressive shape.

artificial fertilizer n

see INORGANIC FERTILIZER.

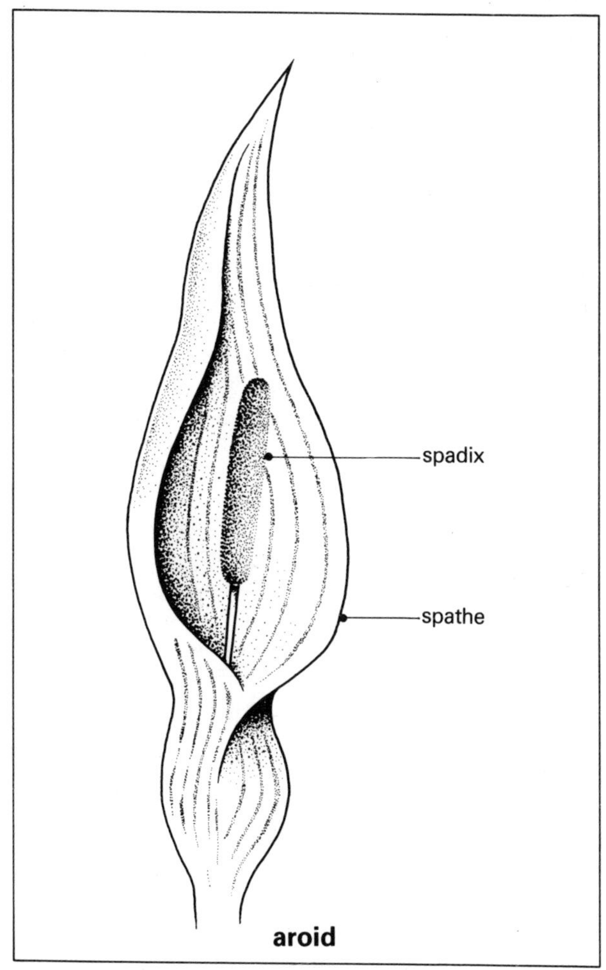

aroid

ascending adj
(of a stem) curving upwards from a more or less horizontal base.

asexual adj
(of a method of propagation) literally, without sex. This term is applied to all forms of VEGATIVE PROPAGATION—ie those that do not involve raising plants from seed.

aspect n
a position facing a particular direction. This term is used to describe the position in which plants may be grown; eg *Hydrangea petiolaris* is suitably grown against a wall with a northern aspect.

attenuate adj
(of a leaf) tapering gradually.

auriculate adj
(of a plant) having ear-like projections. The projections growing at the leaf bases of some grasses are examples of auriculate structures.

auxin n
a substance that in low concentrations stimulates growth, especially by causing shoots to become elongated. Auxin may be a natural plant HORMONE or a man-made product.

awn n
a slender bristle attached to the seeds of some species of grass. Its purpose is to facilitate dispersal of the seed by catching on passing animals or being blown easily in the wind.

axil n
the angle between a branch or leaf and the stem from which it arises.

axillary bud n
a leaf or flower bud arising in an AXIL.

axis n
the main shoot or stem of a plant.

A.Y.R. abb
all year round. This term is usually used in chrysanthemum culture.

back-bulb n
the rearmost and oldest PSEUDOBULB on certain orchids, which can be separated from the parent plant and induced to produce new shoots.

bacterium n, pl **bacteria**
any of a class *(Schizomycetes)* of microscopic organisms that have round, rod-like, spiral or filamentous single-celled bodies and often move by means of whiplike structures called flagella. They live in water, soil, organic matter, or in the bodies of plants and animals and are important because of their chemical effects and because many of them cause diseases.

ball n
the compact mass of roots and soil found in container-grown plants. Also called rootball.

ballbarrow n
a type of wheelbarrow having a large plastic ball in place of a wheel.

balled-and-wrapped adj
(of a tree or shrub) having a good mass of soil around the roots, which is tied and wrapped in sacking or plastic wrapping before a plant is put on sale. Compare BARE-ROOT, CONTAINER-GROWN.

bare-root adj
(of a tree or shrub, etc) having no soil around the roots when sold at the nursery. The roots of such a plant should be well soaked in water before planting.

bark n
the tough exterior covering of a woody root or stem. Processed bark can be used as a fertilizer and soil conditioner.

bark-bound adj
(of a tree) stunted in growth by a lack of moisture or plant foods due to hardening of the tree bark.

bark graft n
a type of graft in which a SCION is inserted under a flap of tree bark. Bark grafting is one method used for FRAMEWORKING of an established tree. Also **bark graft** vt.

[1]**bark-ring** vi
to remove a ring or part of a ring of bark from an apple or pear tree. This is done to restrict growth but also promotes the formation of fruit buds. It is best done in May. Also called knife-ring and ring.

[2]**bark-ring** vt
to treat (a tree) in this way.

basal adj
(of a shoot or bud) growing from the base of a plant.

basal cluster n
a group of leaves, growing close together with very short INTERNODES, at the base of a fruit shoot.

basal cutting n
a young shoot severed at the base of a plant, at or below ground level, and used for PROPAGATION. Dahlias and chrysanthemums are often propagated by basal cuttings.

basal-rooting adj
(of a bulb) rooting only from the base, eg as in most European and American species of lily.

basal stem rot n
see COLLAR ROT.

base n
the lower part of a plant or plant part.

base dressing n
any of various plant foods applied to the soil before planting or sowing crops. See also MULCH. Compare TOP DRESSING.

basic slag n
a chemical fertilizer which contains a slow-releasing PHOSPHATE. Since it also contains lime, it is especially useful on acid soils. Applied during autumn and winter.

bastard trench vt
see DOUBLE DIG.

batter vt
to trim a hedge so that the sides slope inward and the top is narrower than the base. Such a hedge keeps its shape better than one with vertical sides.

bean aphid n
see BLACKFLY.

beard n
a tuft of hair on the lower petals of certain

flowers, particularly some types of iris. Compare CREST.

beaumont period n

a span of 48 hours or longer in which there is high humidity, over 75 per cent, and mild temperatures, over 10°C (50°F). These conditions are associated with encouraging potato blight.

bed n

a plot of ground within a garden especially prepared for plants. See also ISLAND BED and RAISED BED.

bedding perennial n

see ANNUAL.

bedding plant n

any of various plants suitable for growing in garden beds and used for temporary display. These can usually be bought from a nursery when ready for bedding out.

bedding scheme n

a systematic arrangement of bedding plants in a garden; a design.

[1]**bed out** vt

to place (a plant) in a flowering position for display during the summer.

[2]**bed out** vi

to carry out the operation of placing plants for display.

bee n

an insect having a well-defined social organization, often kept in a hive for the honey that it produces; broadly, any of numerous insects that differ from the related wasps especially by having a hairier body and legs, and sometimes a special body structure for carrying pollen. Most bees are the gardener's friend. Insecticides should never be applied to flowering crops as these depend on bees as pollinating agents.

bell-glass n

a bell-shaped glass cover used to protect early vegetable crops.

benomyl n

a SYSTEMIC fungicide effective in the control of a range of diseases, including MILDEW, BOTRYTIS and SCAB. Often sold mixed with THIRAM for seed treatment.

bent-grass n

any of a genus (*Agrostis)* of grasses including important velvety or wiry pasture and lawn grasses.

berry n

a simple fruit in which the seeds are embedded in pulp and protected only by a fleshy outer wall, eg gooseberry. A berry contrasts with a DRUPE, whose seed is enclosed in a hard casing as well as an outer pulp, eg cherry.

BHC abb

benzene hexachloride. See HCH.

bicoloured adj

(of a petal) having two colours.

[1]**biennial** n

a plant that produces leafy growth during its first year and flowers and dies during its second year, eg sweet william and honesty. Biennials are usually sown in late spring or summer, transplanted to a nursery bed in July and transferred to the growing position in autumn or spring. Some PERENNIALS, eg wallflowers, are usuallytreated as biennials.

[2]**biennial** adj

(of a plant) producing leafy growth during its first year and flowering and dying during the second year.

biennial bearing n

a form of CYCLIC BEARING in which a fruit tree produces a crop every other year.

big bud n

any of several diseases of plants (eg blackcurrants) caused by mites and characterized by abnormal swelling of buds, which fail to develop. Spraying with an appropriate chemical should control the condition.

bigeneric adj

(of a hybrid plant) having parents each of which belongs to a different GENUS. Most bigeneric hybrids occur in the orchid and BROMELIAD families. Signified in nomenclature by a cross (X) before the generic name, eg × *Odentonia Olga*

biological control n

the control of pests by introducing their natural predators or parasites to the same site. For example, an infestation of whitefly in a greenhouse can be controlled by introducing the parasitic insect *Encarsia formosa,* whose young feed on whitefly larvae.

bipinnate adj

(of a compound leaf) having branches of

PINNATE leaves that branch from a main leaf stem.

bisexual adj

(of a plant) having both STAMENS and PISTILS in the same flower.

biternate adj

(of a leaf) having three divisions each subdivided into LEAFLETS.

blackfly n

a species of APHID distinguished by its black colour. The insects suck sap from plants such as chrysanthemums, broad beans, runner beans and other vegetables, thus damaging and sometimes killing them. Blackfly can be controlled by spraying with DERRIS, MALATHION, or a SYSTEMIC insecticide. Also known as bean aphid and dolphin fly.

blackleg n

see COLLAR-ROT.

black rot n

a bacterial or fungal disease of plants causing dark brown discoloration and decay.

black spot n

any of several plant diseases characterized by black spots or patches appearing on leaves. Common on roses.

blade n

the flat expanded part of a leaf, as distinguished from its stalk.

blanch vt

to bleach (a growing vegetable) by excluding light and thus preventing the formation of

CHLOROPHYLL. Blanching is done to make vegetables such as celery, leeks and chicory more tender and to improve their taste. The operation can be done by EARTHING-UP, covering the plant with an inverted pot, etc.

bleed vi

(of a plant) to lose an excessive amount of sap after being cut. This is most apparent in spring, when the sap is rising. Vines tend to bleed if they are pruned too near the time of being started into growth.

bleeding n

an abundant loss of sap from severed plant tissues. This is often seen on shrubs and trees pruned late in spring when the sap is rising, and is prevented by early pruning. Bleeding is not harmful to most plants but beetroots can lose a good deal of colour if they are damaged during LIFTING. Bleeding usually stops of its own accord but it can be stopped by applying powdered charcoal or sulphur dust, or sealing the wound with a red-hot iron.

blight n

1 a disease or injury of plants resulting in withering, cessation of growth and death of parts without rotting. **2** an organism, eg an APHID, that causes blight.

blind adj

(of a plant) lacking a TERMINAL growth or flower bud. This is usually caused by physical damage or disease and results in failure to develop properly or death of the plant.

Chrysanthemums and tulips often fail to produce flower buds and are therefore described as blind.

blocking n

a technique for compressing seed and potting composts into small, shaped blocks. Seed is sown directly into the block, thus eliminating the need for a pot. Young plants can then be potted or planted out when roots have developed with little or no disturbance.

[1]**bloom** n

1 a flower. **2** the mass of flowers on a single tree, plant, etc. **3** a delicate powdery or waxy coating on some fruits and leaves.

[2]**bloom** vi

to produce or yield flowers.

[1]**blossom** n

the flower of a plant; especially a flower that produces edible fruits, eg apple blossom.

[2]**blossom** vi

to produce flowers; to bloom.

blossom end rot n

a condition causing tomatoes to develop circular brown patches at the top of newly formed fruit. This is caused by insufficient water and is most likely to appear on plants with a great deal of foliage which takes up the moisture needed by the fruit. It can be prevented by PINCHING OUT; by ensuring that the plant builds up a good root system to take up enough water for both foliage and fruit; and by keeping the soil permanently wet.

blotchy ripening n
a condition causing tomatoes to develop yellow and orange blotches instead of turning their correct colour. This is a result of NITROGEN or POTASSIUM DEFICIENCY and an attack is more likely to be serious if there is inadequate ventilation in the greenhouse.

blue vt
to cause red or pink hydrangeas to turn blue. This is done by planting suitable varieties in a rather ACID compost or by applying 'blueing' chemicals, which contain iron or aluminium sulphate (alum).

bog garden n
an artificial WATER GARDEN used for growing plants which like their roots to be permanently wet. See also BOG PLANT, MARGINAL.

bog moss n
see SPHAGNUM MOSS.

bog plant n
any of various plants that grow in boggy conditions and like their roots to be permanently wet. The water iris and rush are common examples of bog plants.

bole n
the trunk of a tree from ground level to the first branch.

bolt vi
(of a plant) to shoot up to flower before maturing properly. Vegetables such as lettuce and beetroot are particularly likely to bolt, especially in hot, dry weather or in poor soil conditions.

bonemeal n
an organic PHOSPHATE fertilizer made of crushed or ground bone. This is available in fine, medium, and coarse grades. It is slow-acting and ideal for slow-growing crops, shrubs, and HERBACEOUS plants, but the speed with which it acts depends on the soil in which it is used. Its action is faster on light than on heavy soils.

boning rod n
a flat T-shaped wooden stick used as a surveying instrument to level a plot of land. This is 3ft (1m) long, pointed at one end and with a short cross-piece at the other end.

bonsai n
1 a potted shrub or tree dwarfed by artificial restriction of its growth. Stunting is maintained by severe pruning of roots and stems and restriction in a shallow container. Also called dwarf tree. **2** the art of growing and maintaining a dwarfed tree or shrub.

borax n
a chemical compound made up of boron and sodium, used to remedy BORON DEFICIENCY.

Bordeaux mixture n
a mixture of copper sulphate and lime, a useful general-purpose fungicide used to prevent many fungus diseases. It can be bought in powder or paste form ready for mixing with water; once mixed, the preparation must be used immediately.

border n
a narrow bed of planted ground along the edge of a garden, lawn, path etc.

border plant n
any plant suitable for growing in a border.
boron n
a TRACE ELEMENT essential for plant growth.
boron deficiency n
a lack of boron in soil which may cause crops to develop HEART ROT. Applications of BORAX will remedy the deficiency.
botanical adj
(of a plant) occurring more or less unchanged from the original wild form. The term is used particularly of tulips and crocuses.
botanical insecticide n
an insecticide derived from plant material.
botrytis n
any of a group of fungal diseases that cause large areas of a plant to rot. Botrytis is associated with damp conditions and occurs more frequently in winter. It is very difficult to control but spraying with BENOMYL may be beneficial. Also called grey mould.
bottle graft n
a type of APPROACH GRAFT made by cutting the SCION from its parent and placing its base in a bottle of water until the SCION is properly joined to the ROOT-STOCK to which it is grafted. Also **bottle graft** vi.
bottom heat n
heat applied from below, eg to encourage PROPAGATION of plant material. Cuttings root best when the soil is warmer than the air. In greenhouses and frames, an artificial method of

heating the rooting medium is usually necessary. The old method of generating bottom heat was to build a hotbed of freshly fermented MANURE. Modern methods use electric SOIL-WARMING cable buried in the soil, flat metal or plastic plates that enclose a heating element, or hot-water pipes running beneath the propagation bed.

bract n

a modified leaf growing just below the CALYX of a flower. Bracts are often brightly coloured and may be mistaken for petals, as in the poinsettia.

bracteole n

a small or secondary bract.

branch n

a natural division of a plant stem; especially a secondary shoot or stem arising from a main stem or trunk (eg of a tree).

brassica n

any of a large GENUS of temperate-zone plants of the cabbage family, including such vegetables as cabbage, cauliflower, broccoli, brussels sprouts, turnip and rape.

break n

a shoot growing from an AXILLARY BUD, either naturally or artificially. Carnation and chrysanthemum growers PINCH OUT the growing tips of a plant in order to cause break buds to appear, thus promoting bushy growth, but they will also appear naturally on a chrysanthemum left untouched.

break bud n

the bud stage in which bud scales are open just

enough to reveal the green tips of leaves. See also BREAK.

breaking adj
(of a bud stage) referring to the stage when green leaves appear at the apex of a bud.

breastwood n
a group of vigorous shoots that grow forward on mature branches of fruit trees and ornamental shrubs and are difficult to train. These are of no value and should be removed during the summer.

bridge graft n
a graft made to reunite two parts of a tree when the intervening part has been damaged (eg by canker or animals). If such a graft is not made, the branch or tree may be lost. The SCION is of the same variety, preferably thin shoots from the upper part of the tree, and it is inserted so that it bridges the wound. The number of scions will depend on the size of the tree or branch. Also **bridge graft** vt

[1]**broadcast** vt
to scatter (especially seeds) over a wide area.

[2]**broadcast** vi
to sow seeds by scattering them over a wide area rather than placing them in straight lines. Lawn seed is usually sown by broadcasting.

broad-leaved adj
(of trees and shrubs) having broad flat leaves, as opposed to the needle-like leaves of conifers.

broken adj
(of a flower) having an irregular, streaked or blotched pattern, eg as in several varieties of

tulip. The condition is caused by a VIRUS DISEASE but it does not weaken the plant. Also known as feathered or flaked.

bromeliad n

any of a family *(Bromeliaceae)* of chiefly tropical American plants, including the pineapple and various ornamental plants.

brown rot n

a common fungal disease which attacks flower stalks, young shoots and the fruit of many fruit trees including apples, pears, plums, and peaches. The disease causes brownish discolouration and shrivelling. All infected fruit should be destroyed. Brown rot is extremely difficult to control.

brown scale n

a SCALE INSECT which infests the stems of red- and blackcurrants, gooseberries, raspberries, and peaches. Winter spraying with a TAR OIL WASH is the most effective remedy.

brushcutter n

see TRIMMER.

brutting n

1 the breaking of one-year shoots on fruit trees. The shoots are brutted about halfway down so that the end still remains attached to the tree. This is sometimes done to prevent late summer growth, the shoots then being cut back to a few buds below the break in the autumn. **2** the result of treating a fruit tree in this way.

[1]**bud** n

a small protuberance on the stem of a plant that may develop into a flower, leaf or shoot.

[2]**bud** vi

to GRAFT a GROWTH BUD of one plant onto the ROOTSTOCK of another. This is the usual method of propagating roses and some fruit and ornamental trees.

bud-burst adj

(of a bud stage) referring to the stage when the green leaves at the apex of a bud begin to separate.

bud cutting n

see LEAF-BUD CUTTING.

bud-drop n

a condition causing buds to drop before they flower. This is a common condition, and is usually caused by unsuitable conditions or sudden changes of weather. It is less likely to occur if plants are well developed before being allowed to flower.

bud nick vt

to cut (the bark of a fruit tree) beneath a bud in order to keep the bud from bursting. This is done to control the shape in which the tree grows and the cut made is crescent-shaped.

bud notch vt

to cut (the bark of a fruit tree) above a bud in order to stimulate growth. This causes the resulting shoot to grow at a greater angle to the main tree. It is done to control the shape of the tree.

bud rub vi

to remove fruit buds by hand to limit the crop. Buds should be removed at the PINK-BUD stage and the leaves should be left undisturbed.

bud stage n

any of the distinguishable periods of growth and development of a bud. Recognition of the different bud stages is important as they determine when sprays etc, should be applied. See also BREAKING, BUD-BURST, GREEN-CLUSTER, PETAL-FALL, PINK-BUD, SWELLING.

bulb n

1 the short rounded base of the stem of some plants (eg the lily, onion, hyacinth and tulip) that consists of one or more buds enclosed in overlapping fleshy leaves and is usually formed underground as a resting stage in the plant's development. **2** a fleshy plant structure (eg a TUBER or CORM) resembling a bulb in appearance. **3** a plant having or developing from a bulb.

bulb fibre n

a medium consisting of peat, oyster shell and charcoal in which bulbs are grown for indoor decoration. This contains no food material so bulbs grown in it live off the food store within themselves and are exhausted after flowering. They are then no longer fit for indoor cultivation but may be planted outside for another year.

bulb frame n

a special FRAME for keeping certain bulbs dry during their resting period. This is usually of glass with metal edges and is kept entirely closed and unwatered throughout the summer.

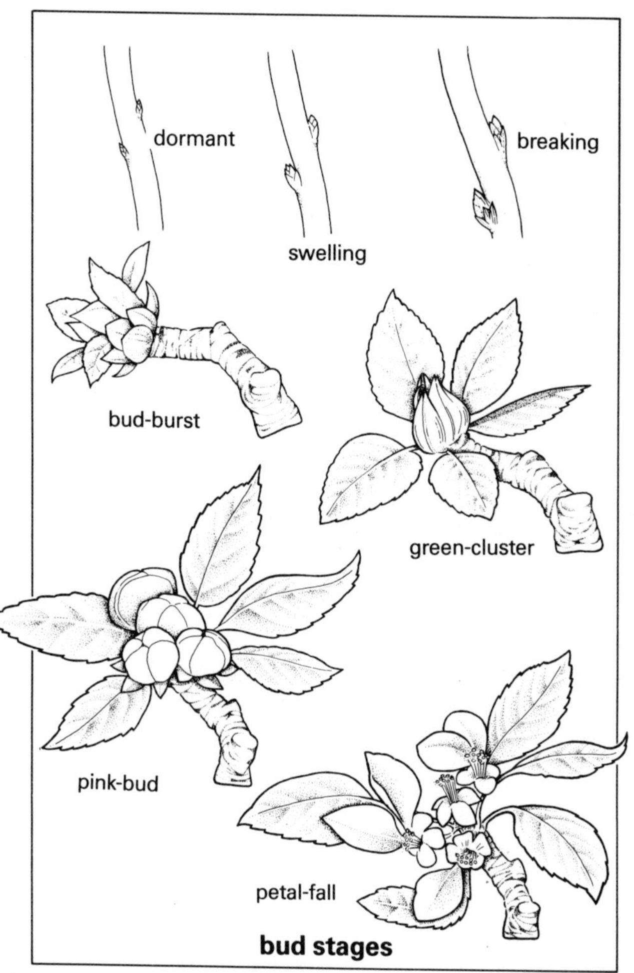
dormant
swelling
breaking
bud-burst
green-cluster
pink-bud
petal-fall

bud stages

bulbil n
a small bulb formed at the side of a mature bulb.
bulblet n
a small aerial bud arising in the axil of the leaves of some plants, eg certain lilies.
bulb planter n
a hand tool with an open cylinder at one end for removing a plug of soil. This is used in planting bulbs, the soil being removed and then replaced once the bulb has been inserted. A bulb planter may have a long or short handle.
bulky adj
(of an organic manure) occupying a large volume of space relative to the food material it contains. Bulky manures not only provide plant food but improve the HUMUS content of the soil.
bulky organic manure n
ORGANIC MANURE which not only has nutritional value but also heavy, substantial material which adds HUMUS to the soil, eg FARMYARD MANURE.
bullate adj
(of a leaf) having a blistered appearance owing to the rising of the main surface above the veins.
bush n
a low, densely-branched shrub. This has no obvious LEADER and its branches arise near the ground.
bush fruit n
see SOFT FRUIT.
bush tree n
a fruit tree whose lowest branches begin no more

than 3 ft (1 m) from the ground.

butterfly n

any of numerous slender-bodied insects (order *Lepidoptera)* that fly by day and have broad, often brightly coloured wings and slender antennae with broad club-shaped ends. The adult is harmless to garden plants but the CATERPILLARS of some kinds of butterfly (eg cabbage large white) can attack plants in the summer and do great damage. Compare MOTH.

cactus n, pl **cacti, cactuses**
any of a family of plants (Cactaceae) that have thick, fleshy stems and SCALES or SPINES instead of leaves, and which occur naturally in deserts and other very dry areas.

caducous adj
(of a plant part) falling off easily, e.g. the petals of some roses.

calcicole n
a plant that usually grows on ALKALINE soil which contains LIME and other CALCIUM compounds. Poppies, scabious and many species of dianthus are calcicoles. Compare CALCIFUGE.

calcifuge n
a plant that dislikes lime and therefore thrives in ACID soil, eg camellia, rhododendron, heather. Such plants are commonly called acid-loving or lime-hating. Compare CALCICOLE.

calcium n
a silver-white chemical element which occurs naturally only in compound forms (eg calcium carbonate). In small quantities it is an essential food for all plants except CALCIFUGES. If a plant is deficient in calcium its leaves will not grow normally, tending to curl inwards, and its

growing points may die. Calcium is normally added to the soil in the form of LIME.

callus n

1 a corky thickening that forms over a wound in the bark of a tree, especially when a limb has been broken off. 2 thickened tissue that forms over the base of a CUTTING before roots are produced.

calomel n

the popular name for mercurous chloride, a poisonous chemical used as both a FUNGICIDE and an INSECTICIDE. This is harmful to fish and should not be used near ponds.

calyx n **calyxes, calyces** pl

the outer, green part of a flower which consists of SEPALS joined together to form a funnel or tube out of which the petals grow.

cambium n

the layer of actively growing tissue just beneath the bark of woody stems. This is responsible for forming the CALLUS and roots on CUTTINGS, healing wounds, and uniting the SCION and ROOTSTOCK in a GRAFT.

campanulate adj

(of a flower) shaped like a bell.

cane n

1 any of various slender woody stems, especially an elongated flowering or fruiting stem (eg of a raspberry), usually growing straight out of the ground. 2 a slender length of reed used as a plant support.

canescent adj
(of a plant part) having a fine covering of greyish-white hairs.

canker n
generally, any of various diseases that cause the bark of trees and shrubs to become cracked and sunken. Canker is caused by many different fungi and bacteria and must be treated immediately. Some attack a range of trees; others are more specific, eg poplar canker. The affected area should be cut out and the wound painted with fungicidal paint. Badly affected plants should be destroyed.

Canterbury hoe n
a hoe with three prongs set at right angles to the handle. This is useful for breaking down rough soil and loosening the surface of hard soil. Also call FORK HOE.

cap vi
(of soil) to form a crust in dry conditions.

capillary action n
the force that results when a liquid is confined in a narrow space, and which has the effect of drawing water up the stem of a plant.

capillary watering n
an automatic watering system used on greenhouse STAGING. Plants in pots and boxes are kept on a permanently moistened layer of sand, from which they extract the water they require by capillary action.

capitate adj
(of a flower) forming a head.

capitulum n
a flowerhead found in some COMPOSITE plants (eg chrysanthemum, dandelion and daisy) in which the AXIS is shortened and dilated to form a rounded or flattened cluster of stalkless flowers, often simulating one larger flower.

capping n
1 the crust that forms on the soil surface in dry conditions. **2** a layer of soil or plastic sheeting placed over a COMPOST HEAP.

capsid bug n
one of a large family of sucking insects which resemble GREENFLY but are more active. They chiefly attack fruit trees and HERBACEOUS plants such as chrysanthemums and dahlias, and rarely go for vegetables or greenhouse plants. Brown-rimmed holes in the plant leaves are a typical symptom. A CONTACT insecticide may be used to control the condition but SYSTEMIC insecticides are more effective.

capsule n
a dry fruit usually containing loose seeds.

captan n
a synthetic fungicide, available as a dust or spray, used to control various fungal diseases, eg apple and pear SCAB and rose BLACK SPOT. It is poisonous to fish and should therefore not be used near ponds.

carpel n
any of the structures of a flowering plant that constitute the female part of a flower, usually consisting of an OVARY, STYLE, and STIGMA.

carpet bedding n
a specialized form of bedding out in which DWARF PLANTS and flat-growing SUCCULENTS are closely spaced to give a continuous carpet-like effect.

catch crop n
a crop of fast-growing vegetables, eg radishes and lettuces, sown and grown to maturity in the period between the harvesting of a main vegetable crop and the planting of another in the same spot. Compare INTERCROP.

caterpillar n
the elongated wormlike LARVA of a butterfly or moth. Caterpillars are common garden pests: most species feed on leaves but some feed on roots and others tunnel into stems and fruit. They can be controlled by hand-picking and spraying with insecticides such as MALATHION and DERRIS.

catkin n
a flower SPIKE, often pendulous, which is composed of densely crowded BRACTS, each of which surrounds one or more stalkless, unisexual flowers without petals. Willow, hazel and birch trees all bear catkins.

caudate adj
(of a leaf apex) resembling a tail.

cell n
the basic unit of all plant tissue, consisting of a nucleus embedded in protoplasm and cell sap, surrounded by a semipermeable membrane.

centipede n
any of a class of long flattened many-segmented

invertebrate animals with each segment bearing one pair of legs. They are brown in colour and live on minute soil animals. Unlike MILLEPEDES they do not attack garden plants.

certified stock n

a fruit or vegetable ROOTSTOCK that has been certified by the Ministry of Agriculture as being true to name and free from certain diseases.

chafer beetle n

any of various large beetles whose fat white larvae live in soil and do great damage to the roots and crowns of plants. They may be controlled by raking a CONTACT insecticide into the soil at any time of year. The adult beetles eat holes in leaves but cause only superficial damage.

chalk n

a soft white, grey, or buff limestone composed chiefly of the shells of small marine organisms. Consisting of calcium carbonate or carbonate of lime, this is convertible into quicklime by burning in a kiln. Ground chalk is useful for improving texture: it opens up clay soils and makes light soils more able to retain moisture. It also corrects soil acidity. The more finely ground the chalk is, the quicker its effect in the garden will be. So-called lime-hating plants, such as rhododendrons and azaleas, cannot thrive in soil containing too much chalk. Other plants, such as poppies and species of dianthus, love chalk. Naturally chalky soils often benefit from a dressing of MANURE, PEAT and LEAF MOULD. See also CALCICOLE, CALCIFUGE.

chalky adj
see ALKALINE.

channelled adj
(of a narrow leaf) having upturned margins that form a hollowed, gutter-like shape.

charcoal n
a dark or black porous carbon prepared by partly burning vegetable or animal substances, such as wood or bone. This is often used in small lumps as an ingredient in potting composts, in which it facilitates drainage and keeps the soil sweet by absorbing gases. It is always used in BULB FIBRE and is valuable for orchids and slow-growing plants. Charcoal contains no nutrients.

chelated compound n
see SEQUESTRENE.

Cheshunt Compound trademark
a fungicid containing SULPHATE OF COPPER and ammonium carbonate, used to control DAMPING-OFF in seedlings. This should be applied as GERMINATION takes place and can be used either as a preventive measure before damping-off appears, or as a control where the fungus has already appeared.

chimaera n
see MUTANT.

Chinese layering n
see AIR LAYERING.

chip vt
to break the outer coat of a seed to hasten germination. This is done by nicking the seed with a knife or rubbing it with sandpaper.

Chipping is useful with hard seeds such as those of lupins or sweet peas.

chit vi
to germinate or sprout.

chlordane n
a highly poisonous insecticide, based on the element chlorine, which exists as a liquid and is used as an ingredient in several proprietary powders.

chlorophyll n
the green colouring matter in plants. Its function is to act with sunlight and bring about the elaborate series of chemical changes (PHOTOSYNTHESIS) in plant leaves which produces plant growth.

chlorosis n
the loss of CHLOROPHYLL in a leaf which causes the leaf to turn yellow and may kill the plant. This is usually caused by a lack of essential minerals in the soil but may be caused by a virus.

chromosome n
any of many rod-like bodies in a plant cell which carry the genetic characteristics of the plant.

chrysalis n, pl **chrysalides, chrysalises**
the inactive stage of development of an insect between LARVA and adult. The term is used particularly of moths, beetles and butterflies at this stage. Also known as PUPA.

ciliate adj
(of a leaf) fringed with fine hairs or bristles.

circle n

see WHORL.

cirrhose adj

(of a leaf apex) having a curl-like filament.

cladode n

a plant stem having the form of and closely resembling an ordinary foliage leaf and often bearing leaves or flowers on its edges, eg in certain types of broom. Compare PHYLLOCLADE, PHYLLODE.

clamp n

a place where root crops (eg potatoes, carrots and turnips) can be stored outdoors. The vegetables are piled in a cone-shaped heap and covered first with a thick layer of straw and then another of soil to keep out frosts. A 'chimney' of straw in the top of the clamp provides ventilation. Also called pie.

clasping adj

see AMPLEXICAUL.

classification n

the system of arranging plants in classes and giving them names that are understood and accepted throughout the world. Latin names are preferred to common names because the latter are imprecise; also, two or more plants can share a common name, and one plant can have different common names in different areas. Plants are classified according to family, genus, species and variety.

The genus (pl genera) is similar to a surname and comprises a group of plants that are similar in structure and supposed to be descended from a common ancestor. When a plant is named in full, the genus name is always placed first and has a capitalized initial letter, eg *Cheiranthus*. When a genus name is used frequently in writing, it may be abbreviated to its single first letter after the first mention: eg, *Cheiranthus* to *C*. A genus may also be described by a popular name: *Cheiranthus* is also known as wallflower.

Related genera make up a family, eg the genera of calendula and Chrysanthemum are members of the *Compositae* family. The genus C*heiranthus* is a member of the *Cruciferae* family.

The genus is the basic unit and may encompass a number of species with similar structures, mainly of flower, fruit and seed. When a plant is named in full, the species name is placed second and has a small initial letter, eg *Cheiranthus cheiri*.

If a number of distinct forms occur naturally within a species, that species may be subdivided into varieties. The name of the variety is given in Latin and comes after the name of the species, sometimes after the abbreviation 'var', eg *Clematis montana var rubens* or simply *Clematis montana rubens*. Cultivated varieties produced by hybridization are called cultivars (*abb* c.v.). They are not normally given Latin names but names chosen by the breeder and placed inside inverted commas, eg *Tagetes erecta* 'Spun Gold', or *Cheiranthus cheiri* 'Orange Bedder'.

A hybrid is a plant resulting from the

interbreeding of two species from the same genus. It is given a Latin name and prefixed by a multiplication sign, eg *Freesia* × *kewensis* is a hybrid species between *Freesia refracta* and *Freesia armstrongii*. See also BIGENERIC.

clay n
an earth material that is pliable when moist and composed mainly of fine particles of aluminium silicates and other minerals. The more clay there is in a soil, the harder it is to cultivate. It is not FRIABLE; it tends to become waterlogged in wet weather and to bake hard in hot weather. Clay soils are often highly fertile, however, and their texture can be improved by adding MANURE, PEAT, LEAF MOULD and coarse sand. Proprietary conditioners (usually based on gypsum) designed to improve clay soils are also available. Over the years, such treatment will greatly improve the quality of the soil.

cleft adj
(of a leaf margin) indented about halfway to the MIDRIB.

cleft graft n
a type of graft in which SCIONS are inserted into the stump of a headed-back branch for the purpose of FRAMEWORKING an old or cut-back tree. Also **cleft graft** vt.

climber n
1 strictly, any plant that climbs up a firm surface attaching itself to the surface as it does so by special means, eg AERIAL ROOTS, little adhesive pads on the ends of TENDRILS, or twining stems.

Ivy, clematis and Russian vine are all true climbers, as distinct from erect plants that can be trained against walls or trellises but do not actually attach themselves. **2** loosely, any plant that climbs towards the light, attaching itself or being trained against a wall or trellis, eg clematis, honeysuckle, pyracantha. Also called creeper.

cloche n

a translucent cover, usually of plastic or glass, used for warming up soil in early spring and protecting plants. Crops protected with cloches can be sown earlier in the year than those not protected. Cloches are light, easy to carry and can be moved quickly from one crop to another.

clod n

a lump or mass of soil.

clone n

a plant obtained from a single parent plant by VEGETATIVE PROPAGATION. Clones always carry genetic information identical to that of the parent plant.

close adj

1 *(of a greenhouse or frame)* shut up and unventilated. **2** *(of a greenhouse atmosphere)* humid and unventilated. A close atmosphere is useful for rooting CUTTINGS.

clove n

1 a small individual BULB forming part of a cluster, eg in young shallots or garlic. **2** a strongly-scented species of carnation.

club root n
a serious disease caused by a soil fungus which attacks members of the *Cruciferae* family (eg brassicas, wallflowers and stocks), causing their roots to become swollen and distorted. The disease is especially likely to occur in acid, badly drained soils. Affected plants should be destroyed. Applications of CALOMEL help prevent the disease, as does adequate liming of the soil. Also known as finger and toe.

cockchafer n
a common type of CHAFER BEETLE. Both the adult beetle and the LARVA cause extensive damage to plants. They are not easy to control but certain insecticides (eg HCH) can be effective. Also known as May bug.

cold frame n
a FRAME, usually glass-covered, without artificial heat used to protect plants and seedlings.

cold house n
an unheated greenhouse.

collar n
loosely, the part of a plant where the roots join the stems.

collar rot n
any of various fungal diseases that attack plant stems at the base, causing blackening and decay. The diseases include basal stem rot, blackleg and DAMPING-OFF. They are most likely to occur when the soil around the stem is kept too wet and they cannot be cured. Also known as neck rot.

colour border n

a HERBACEOUS BORDER planted with flowers of only one or two colours.

colour break n

a form of MUTATION in chrysanthemums that causes their colours to change.

column n

a flower organ (eg of an orchid) formed by the fusion of male and female reproductive organs. See also GYNANDROUS.

composite adj

(of a flowering plant) relating to or being of the plant family *Compositae*. The composite plants include such familiar species as the dandelion and daisy. Often considered the most highly evolved of all plants, they are characterized by many small FLORETS arranged in dense heads resembling single flowers.

compost n

1 a MANURE substitute produced from rotted-down garden and kitchen refuse. See also COMPOST HEAP. **2** a complete growing medium used for raising seedlings and for growing plants in pots and containers. Proprietary composts are of two main types: one has soil as its main ingredient (see JOHN INNES COMPOST), the other has peat (see SOILLESS COMPOST).

compost bin n

a wooden, metal or plastic container used to hold a COMPOST HEAP of rotting-down garden and kitchen refuse. It is possible to buy a compost bin for making compost; alternatively, a container

composite flowers

can be made out of wooden slats, a perforated plastic dustbin, or wire mesh sealed with a perforated plastic liner.

compost heap n

a pile of organic material used for producing home-made MANURE substitute. This provides FERTILIZER for the garden soil and a disposal method for household and garden refuse. Compost can be made from any vegetable wastes but diseased material, wood, and the roots of any PERENNIAL WEED should be avoided. Tough material, eg cabbage stalks, should be cut into pieces about 2 in (5 cm) long. The compost heap should be built up in layers over a 3 in (7.5 cm) base layer of coarse material such as brushwood, hedge trimmings and broken bricks, to ensure good drainage and aeration. The other layers should be about 6 in (15 cm) thick and composed of diverse types of waste. If dry, the material should be saturated with water and then sprinkled with an ACCELERATOR to speed up the decaying process. To stimulate bacterial activity, other forms of NITROGEN may be added to the compost via poultry or animal manure, SULPHATE OF AMMONIA or concentrated seaweed extract. When the pile has reached a height of about 4 ft (1.2 m), it is covered with a perforated plastic sheet; this should in turn be covered with an insulating layer of soil, old straw, or sacks. The resulting compost is ready to use in about six months, when it should be moist and crumbly and have no unpleasant smell. The original materials should not be recognizable.

A simpler method of making a compost heap is just to pile the vegetable matter into a heap, cover it with a plastic sheet and allow it to decompose on its own. Compost made in this way will not be ready for use for at least a year.

Compost can be used as a manure and applied at about 2–3 buckets per square yard (square metre). This should be done annually and the compost should be worked into the soil thoroughly when digging. Alternatively it may be spread in a layer on the surface of the soil, when worms will work it in naturally. It can also be used as a TOP DRESSING round plants to retain moisture and to prevent roots getting scorched.

compound adj

(of a leaf, flower or fruit) composed of several united, similar elements. Common examples are rose leaves, daisy flowers, and strawberry fruit.

compound fertilizer n

a fertilizer that incorporates the most essential nutrients for soil—ie PHOSPHORUS, POTASSIUM, and NITROGEN. Proprietary brands are available, of which some are for specific plants (eg rose fertilizer) and others for general garden use. Compound fertilizers can be used either as a base dressing or as a top dressing.

condensation n

the water formed when warm, moist air comes into contact with a cold surface. It forms under glass covering a box of seedlings or on the inside surfaces of a cloche, frame or greenhouse. Glass covering for seedlings should be wiped daily to avoid DAMPING-OFF.

conducting system n

the vascular organization of a plant which enables it to carry out life processes.

cone n

the fruit of a conifer, usually composed of overlapping woody scales that are arranged on an axis and bear seeds between them.

conifer n

any of various orders of mostly evergreen trees and shrubs, including pine, cypress and yew, that bear their seeds in cones.

connate adj

(*of plant parts*) congenitally or firmly united.

conservatory n

a greenhouse, usually forming an extension to a house, in which ornamental plants are grown and displayed.

contact adj

(*of a pesticide*) designed to kill garden pests on contact. Compare SYSTEMIC.

container-grown adj

(*of a plant*) grown in a pot or other container, as distinct from a plant grown in open ground and then lifted and transplanted for garden use. Container-grown plants can be planted out in any season because the roots will hardly be disturbed in the process.

contractile adj

(*of bulb or corm roots*) having the power to

contract, thereby pulling a bulb or corm deeper into the soil.

controlled-release adj
see SLOW-RELEASE.

copper n
a naturally occurring metallic element which is a TRACE ELEMENT essential for plant growth.

copper fungicide n
any of various fungicides based on copper compounds, available in powder, liquid and dust form. These are used to control a variety of diseases, eg potato BLIGHT or RUST.

coral spot n
a fungal disease, usually affecting dead wood, which shows itself as small coral-pink pustules. Infected wood should be cut out and burnt.

[1]**coppice** vt
to cut back (a group of trees) in order to produce a dense growth of small trees.

[2]**coppice** n
a thicket, grove or growth of small trees.

cordate adj
(of a leaf) heart-shaped.

cordon n
1 a fruit tree or shrub, usually apple, pear or gooseberry, specially trained and pruned to produce fruit on a single stem or only a few stems. Fruit trees grown as cordons are particularly suitable for small gardens because they give a high yield relative to the amount of space they take up. Double or triple cordons are plants restricted to two or three main stems

respectively. **2** any plant artificially restricted to a single stem, eg cordon sweet peas are those in which all side shoots have been removed.

coriaceous adj

(of a leaf) tough and leathery to the touch.

corm n

a rounded, thick underground stem base with buds and scaly leaves, that stores food and produces new shoots each year (eg in the crocus). Compare BULB, TUBER.

cormel n

a small or secondary CORM produced by a larger corm. Also known as a cormlet.

cormlet n

see CORMEL.

corolla n

the ring of petals forming the inner envelope of a flower, usually brightly coloured to attract pollinating insects.

corona n

the cup or trumpet of a flower, eg of a daffodil or narcissus, which lies between the stamens and the petals.

cottage garden n

a garden of a type supposedly typical of country cottages in the nineteenth and early twentieth centuries, devoted mainly to vegetables, herbs and informal borders of annual and biennial ornamental plants (eg hollyhocks, wallflowers and chrysanthemums).

corymb n

a flat-topped flower cluster in which the flower

stalks arise at different levels on the main axis and reach approximately the same height, and in which the outer flowers open first.

cotyledon n

the first seed leaf or one of the first pair of leaves to appear at the GERMINATION of a seed. Cotyledons are contained in the seed before germination and are often different in shape from a plant's adult leaves. See also DICOTYLEDON, MONOCOTYLEDON.

cover crop n

see GREEN MANURE.

creeper n

1 strictly, any plant that spreads over the ground, rooting as it does so. **2** loosely, any CLIMBER.

crenate adj

(of a leaf margin) having shallow notches forming rounded scallops.

crenulate adj

(of a leaf margin) having an irregularly wavy or serrated outline.

creosote n

a clear or yellowish oily liquid mixture of chemical compounds, obtained from wood tar and used especially as an antiseptic or disinfectant. Though an excellent wood preservative, it is no longer much used in gardens since its fumes are harmful to plants over a long period.

crest n

1 a showy tuft of hairs or soft bristles found on the lower petals of some species of iris. Compare BEARD. **2** a flattened or spreading growth, usually at the top of a plant, which is an abnormal feature caused by FASCIATION.

crested adj

see CRISTATE.

crinkle n

any of several plant diseases marked by a crinkling of the leaves.

crisped adj

(of a plant organ) having a closely curved or finely waved margin.

cristate adj

(of a plant) literally, having a crest. This term is applied to plants with FASCIATION forming a type of crest. Also called crested.

crop rotation n

see ROTATION.

crock n

a piece of broken earthenware, used in gardening to cover the hole at the bottom of a flowerpot so as to facilitate drainage. Crocks are unnecessary in plastic flowerpots with several drainage holes.

cross n

see HYBRID.

cross-fertilization n

see CROSS-POLLINATION.

cross-pollination n

the transfer of pollen from the anther (pollen-producing organ) of one flower to the stigma (pollen-receiving organ) of another flower on a separate plant.Compare SELF-POLLINATION.

crotch n

an angle formed where two branches separate off

from the trunk of a tree. Also called crutch.

crown n

1 the junction of root and stem in a HERBACEOUS perennial at soil level or just below. Peonies and rhubarb, for example, die back to the crown each autumn and form resting bulbs just below the surface. **2** the roots of rhubarb lifted for FORCING. **3** the upper part of the foliage of a tree or shrub.

crown bud n

the main central flower at the tip of a shoot.

crown gall n

a plant disease caused by a bacterium which forms tumorous swellings just below the ground on the trunk and stem. The plants usually affected are fruit and shrubs.

crown graft n

a type of graft used in TOPWORKING an old fruit tree, in which the tree is headed back and several SCIONS are inserted into the rind or ring of bark on the stump. Also called rind graft. Also

crown graft vt.

crown lift vt

to remove the lower branches of a tree in order to make the trunk more visible, or to remove branches that are dead or obstructive.

crucifer n

any plant of the cabbage family, including wallflowers, mustard and honesty.

[1]**crown thin** vi

to remove selected tree branches in order to avoid

crowding and to let in more air and light to the CROWN.

[2]**crown thin** vt

to use this method of thinning on (a stand of trees).

cruciform adj

(of a plant part) arranged in a cross, like the petals of a wallflower.

crutch n

see CROTCH.

cuckoo spit n

a frothy mass secreted on plants by the CUCKOO-SPIT INSECT.

cuckoo-spit insect n

the LARVA of the FROGHOPPER. This lives in a frothy secretion which it deposits on a plant from which it sucks sap, causing leaves to wilt and shoots to malform. It is not a serious pest and can be controlled with an insecticide such as MALATHION or HCH.

cultivar n

a plant that has been originated in and kept under cultivation, as opposed to in the wild. See also CLASSIFICATION.

cultivate vt

1 to prepare or use (soil) for the growing of crops. **2** to loosen or break up the soil around (growing plants).

cultivator n

a garden tool used to loosen or break up soil, often around growing plants. Cultivators vary in size and sophistication from a long-handled instrument with 3 or 5 curved prongs, operated by hand, to a wheel-mounted, power-operated machine used to plough up land in the early stages of garden construction.

cuneate adj
(of a leaf) wedge-shaped.

cupule n
the cup-shaped fruit-bearing structure of some plants, eg the cup in which an acorn sits.

curd n
the edible head of a plant, eg cauliflower or broccoli.

cushion-forming plant n
see CUSHION PLANT.

cushion plant n
a small plant shaped as a cushion-like mound, eg many ALPINES and certain types of saxifrage. Also known as a cushion-forming plant.

cuspidate adj
(of a leaf) having a pointed end.

cut back vt
to shorten (branches of trees and shrubs) by cutting. See also PRUNE.

cuticle n
a thin waxy film of CUTIN coating the external surfaces of many plants.

cutin n
a water-repellent substance containing waxes and fats that becomes impregnated into plant cell walls and forms a continuous layer on the external surface of plants.

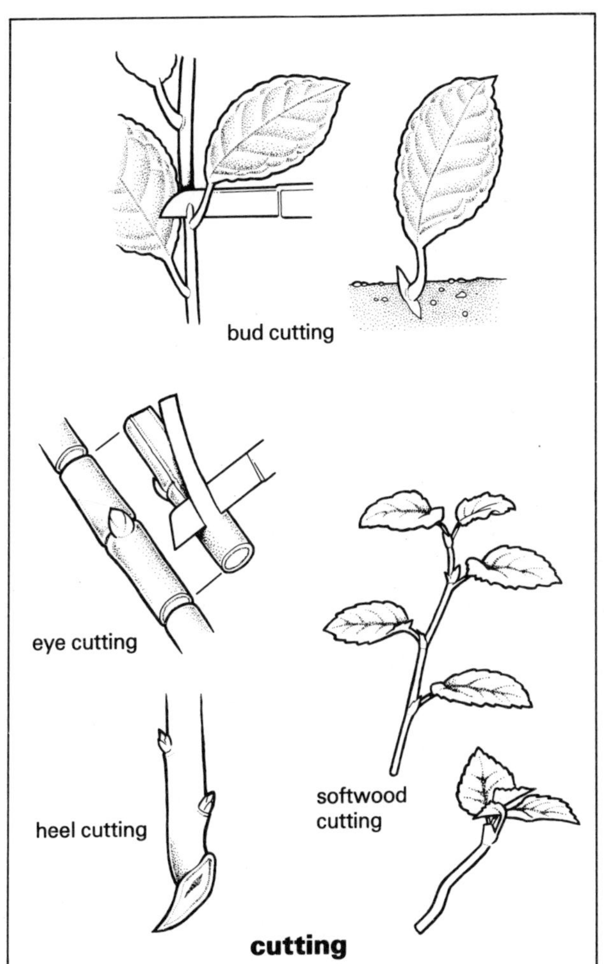

cutting

cutting

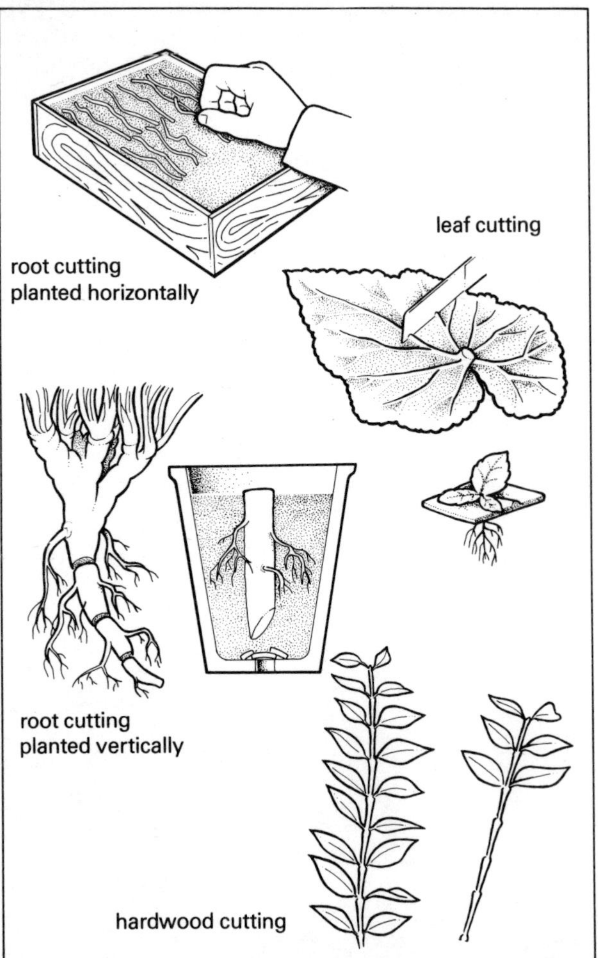
root cutting
planted horizontally
leaf cutting
root cutting
planted vertically
hardwood cutting

cut-leaved adj
(of a tree or shrub) having leaves that are deeply cut into narrow segments.

cutting n
any part of a living plant, such as a section of stem, leaf, root or bud, removed and treated in such a way as to be capable of becoming a new plant.

cutworm n
any of various CATERPILLARS active chiefly at night, many of which feed on plant stems near ground level. These are not easily controlled because their presence is usually detected only after damage has been done, but they can be killed by watering the soil with HCH.

cyclic bearing n
a habit of certain plants of producing fruit at intervals of more than one year. See also BIENNIAL BEARING.

cylinder mower n
see LAWN MOWER.

cyme n
a flower cluster in which each side stem ends in a single flower. The main flower stem usually bears the central and first-opening flower with subsequent flowers developing from side stems. See also INFLORESCENCE.

cymose adj
being or bearing a CYME.

dalapon n
a SELECTIVE WEEDKILLER used to control ANNUAL and PERENNIAL grasses. Uncropped land should not be used for weeks after treatment.

damp down vt
to wet the floor, walls and STAGING of (a greenhouse) in order to increase humidity and lower temperature. Compare DAMP OVERHEAD.

damping-off n
a common disease mainly of young seedlings grown under glass in which rotting of the stem occurs at ground level. This is caused by a number of fungi and the result is that the seedlings topple and die. Damping-off can spread rapidly in badly ventilated growing conditions and crowded sowings. It can be prevented by watering the compost with CHESHUNT COMPOUND or by dusting the seed boxes with a proprietary seed dressing.

damp overhead vt
to spray greenhouse plants, their pots and STAGING with water in order to cover them with a layer of moisture. This should not be done in greenhouses that receive direct sunlight, as SCORCHING could occur, and ample air should

always be admitted to prevent disease. Compare DAMP DOWN.

day-neutral adj
(of a plant) able to flower regardless of the length of daylight (strictly, length of darkness), eg pansy. Compare LONG-DAY; SHORT-DAY.

[1]**dead-head** vt
to remove dead flower heads from (a plant). This is done to prevent the plant from setting seed; to ensure a succession of blooms on shrubs (eg roses) throughout the summer; and to keep the garden tidy.

[2]**dead-head** n
a dead flowerhead.

deblossom vt
to remove flowers from (a fruit tree). This is usually done in a tree's first year after planting to give it a chance to establish itself without having to produce fruit. Older trees are sometimes partially deblossomed if the quantity of blossom is enormous and if the previous year's crop was light. This is done to prevent BIENNIAL BEARING.

deciduous adj
(of a plant) losing all leaves at the end of the growing season. The term is used especially of trees and shrubs. Deciduous plants should normally only be planted or transplanted when they are leafless. Compare EVERGREEN.

decumbent adj
(of a plant) having stems growing flat on the

ground but rising into the air at the tip. Compare PROCUMBENT.

decurrent adj

(of a leaf) having a base that extends downwards on its stalk or on the plant stem.

decussate adj

(of leaves) arranged in pairs, each at right angles to the next pair above or below.

deep bed n

a bed, especially one intended for growing vegetables, which is initially double dug and heavily composted or manured but is not subsequently dug or compacted.

deficiency disease n

any plant disease caused by a lack of essential nutrients. See BORON DEFICIENCY, MANGANESE DEFICIENCY, NITROGEN DEFICIENCY, POTASH/POTASSIUM DEFICIENCY.

defoliate vt

to remove unwanted leaves from (a plant) in order to prevent disease.

defruit vt

to remove immature fruit from (a fruit tree). This is usually done if DEBLOSSOMING was not carried out in time.

dehisce vi

(of fruits and anthers) to discharge seeds and pollen by splitting along natural seams.

dehorn vt

to prune (an old fruit tree) by removing some or all of the larger branches. This is slightly less severe than HEADING BACK.

deltoid adj

(of a leaf) triangular.

dendrology n

the study of trees.

dentate adj

(of a leaf) having tooth-like projections along the margins.

derris n

a botanical insecticide originating from the roots of a tropical plant of the same name. Its active ingredient is ROTENONE. This has a relatively low toxicity to humans but it is deadly to fish and should never be used near a pond. Derris is not as effective as many synthetic insecticides but it is of value where the use of HCH would be unwise.

deshoot vt

to remove very young shoots from (trained trees). This is sometimes referred to as to disbud, but that term should be applied only to the removal of blossom buds.

determinate adj

(of a plant) having a stem that ends in a flower bud or TRUSS, as opposed to growing indefinitely. Compare INDETERMINATE.

dibber n

a tool with a blunt point used for making holes in the soil when transplanting seedlings. Dibbers are usually made of wood or metal and vary in size from pencil-sized sticks to thick pegs with handles. Also called DIBBLE.

dibble n

see DIBBER.

dichlofluanid n

a sulphur-based fungicide used to control BOTRYTIS on tomatoes and lettuce plants.

dicotyledon n

any of a group of flowering plants that have two cotyledons, or seed leaves, formed when the plant begins to grow from seed. Compare MONOCOTYLEDON.

dieback n

a condition causing the death of young shoots. This can affect many plants, and can follow frost damage or may be caused by a parasitic fungus which enters through a wound. Infected shoots should be cut back and the wounds coated with protective paint.

dig vt

to break up, turn or loosen (soil) with a spade or fork. Digging is essential for the creation and maintenance of fertile soil, and should be carried out in the autumn so that frost and rain during the winter will break down the soil even more. Manure and compost can be incorporated at the same time. See also DOUBLE DIG, SINGLE DIG, TRENCH.

digitate adj

(of a leaf) having leaflets arranged like the fingers of a hand and growing from the top of the stem stalk.

dimethoate n

a SYSTEMIC insecticide used to kill sap-sucking

insects. This can be mixed with other insecticides for effective control of other garden pests. It is not highly toxic but crops should not be harvested until at least one week after application.

dinocap n

a fungicide used to control POWDERY MILDEW which attacks roses, gooseberries, etc.

dioecious adj

(of a plant species) having male and female flowers on different plants. FERTILIZATION and the production of fruit can only be ensured on certain plants, eg most forms of skimmia and holly, if a male plant is planted among female plants.

diploid adj

(of a plant) having the full number of CHROMOSOMES characteristic of the species. See also TETRAPLOID and TRIPLOID.

diplostemenous adj

(of a flower) having STAMENS on alternating WHORLS.

diquat n

a powerful inorganic weedkiller similar to PARAQUAT.

disbud vt

1 to remove surplus buds and shoots from (a plant) in order to encourage an exhibition-size flower. This is often done to chrysanthemums and is sometimes referred to as 'securing the bud'. **2** to remove growth buds from (young fruit trees) in order to create a desired shape.

disk, disc n
the domed centre of any flower of the daisy family, consisting of many tiny TUBULAR FLORETS.

dissected adj
(of a leaf or petal) deeply cut into several fine lobes.

distichous adj
(of a leaf) having parts arranged in two vertical rows, creating a fan-like effect.

distributor n
a mechanical device used to spread any type of material, eg fertilizer, on a lawn.

division n
1 one of the simplest forms of plant PROPAGATION, effected by dividing plant parts and planting those segments capable of producing roots and shoots. This is carried out during the winter or at the beginning of the new growing season, and is the easiest way of increasing many PERENNIAL plants. The roots of the plant are lifted and divided into pieces, each of which is then replanted separately to produce a new plant. **2** a rooted segment of plant removed for propagation.

dolphin fly n
see BLACKFLY.

dormant adj
1 *(of a plant)* temporarily ceasing to grow during the autumn and winter. See also RESTING PERIOD. **2** *(of a bud)* inactive unless stimulated into growth by pruning or by accidental removal

of other, active shoots. Also known as latent.

dorsal adj

(of a plant) literally, of, being, or situated on the surface of a plant structure that faces away from the central axis. This term is applied to the middle SEPAL of orchid flowers, the one which stands upright and is most noticeable.

dot plant n

a tall, conspicuous plant used in a formal bedding scheme to provide a contrast in height, shape, or colour with smaller plants.

double adj

(of a flower) having more than the usual number of petals for that species, eg dahlias, carnations, and paeonies. The extra petals are usually PETALOID. Compare SINGLE, SEMI-DOUBLE.

double cordon n

see CORDON.

double dig vt

to dig (soil) to a depth of two SPITS. Soil that has been neglected for a long time should be double dug before being planted; cultivated soil should be double dug every three years. Also called bastard trench, half trench. Compare SINGLE DIG, TRENCH.

double-leader adj

(of a tree) having twin vertical shoots rather than one at the top.

downy mildew n

a condition caused by various fungi, which causes leaves to turn yellow on the upper side and a greyish mould to form on the underside. It is difficult to control but careful spraying with fungicide may help prevent it. Plants such as sweet pea and poppy are particularly susceptible. Compare POWDERY MILDEW.

drag brush n
a brush-like tool with a long handle designed to be pulled across turf to work in a TOP DRESSING.

drag fork n
a fork with broad tines bent at right angles to the handle.

drainage n
a method or system used to ensure that rainwater is drawn away gradually, so that the soil does not become waterlogged.

Any site where plants grow must be well drained: if it is not, the result will be dead roots, poor growth, and perhaps even dead plants. Most garden soil can be kept properly drained by the regular addition of bulky organic materials such as PEAT or LEAF-MOULD. But if there is a tendency for the soil to get waterlogged anyway, 3-in (7.5-cm) drainpipes can be placed 2 ft (60 cm) down in the soil, and they should lead to a proper outlet.

Soil near a wall is always relatively dry so plants should be planted at least 12 in (30 cm) away rather than right up against it.

drainage trench n
a deep, narrow excavation in the ground for carrying excess water from part of a garden.

draw vi
to make a seed DRILL with a hoe.

draw hoe n
a hoe with a broad flat blade set at right angles to the handle, which is often swan-necked. As the name implies, this is usually drawn towards the user, rather than being pushed backwards and forwards like a Dutch hoe. This is useful for breaking up rough ground and for drawing up soil to EARTH-UP vegetables.

drawn adj
(of a plant or seedling) unnaturally long, thin, and pale in colour. Plants become drawn when they are overcrowded and lack sufficient light.

drench vt
to apply liquid pesticide to the roots of (a plant).

dribble bar n
a perforated bar that fits onto the spout of a watering can and allows weedkiller, etc, to be applied precisely and at a constant rate.

dried blood n
a long-lasting organic fertilizer containing 13 per cent NITROGEN. It is expensive for outdoor use but is useful as a TOP DRESSING for greenhouse plants.

drill n
a shallow furrow into which seed is sown. It is usually made by drawing a rake or hoe through the soil.

drought n
a continuous period of at least fifteen days without rain.

drupe n
a fruit having usually a single seed enclosed in a hard stony coat and surrounded by juicy flesh and a thin flexible or stiff coat. There are two types: cherries, plums, etc, are simple drupes; blackberries, raspberries, etc, are compound drupes.

dry set n
a condition of tomato flowers in which the OVARY dries up and does not grow to form a normal fruit. It is caused by faulty POLLINATION and usually occurs when the atmosphere is too dry.

duster n
a mechanical device used for scattering powdered insecticide or fungicide over crops. The simplest duster is similar to bellows and expels the powder when shaken; a more complicated type distributes the powder by use of a fan.

Dutch hoe n
a hoe with a long narrow blade set at almost the same plane as the handle. This is used by moving the blade backwards and forwards just below the surface of the soil, and is useful for keeping down weeds.

Dutch light n
a single sheet of glass, of specific measurements, surrounded by a simple wooden frame. A Dutch light may be used singly to make a cold frame, or a number can be built up on a structure to create a Dutch light greenhouse.

dwarf vt
to hinder or arrest the growth or develpment of (a plant). Also called stunt.

dwarf plant n
1 loosely, any plant that is naturally very small.
2 a plant whose growth has been restricted deliberately so that it is below normal size. Many varieties of shrubs and trees, eg conifers, are dwarfed to make them suitable for small gardens, and dwarf forms of HERBACEOUS plants, eg delphiniums, have been developed by breeders and are very popular. When such plants have been developed by breeding, their seeds continue the dwarf size. They contrast with other dwarf plants, such as the BONSAI, whose development has been stunted by careful and deliberate pruning etc, and will not be carried on to another generation.

dwarf tree n
see BONSAI.

earth-up vt
to draw up a mound of soil around (a plant). The mound is formed at the plant stem, usually with a hoe or spade, and given sloping sides for good drainage. This technique is used for different purposes with different types of plant: eg celery and chicory are earthed up to BLANCH them; brussels sprouts and broccoli are earthed up to protect them from wind. With potatoes the technique encourages formation of TUBERS and protects the tubers from frost damage and potato blight; it also prevents them turning green and bitter through exposure to light. Also known as hill-up.

earwig n
an elongated brownish insect, commonly a garden pest. It can damage the leaves and flowers of certain plants, particularly dahlias. To control earwigs, plants should be dusted or sprayed with HCH.

edge vt
to trim (the edges of a lawn) with suitable tool, eg a spade, edger or long-handled shears.

edger n
a tool used to trim the edges of a lawn. A typical

form is a rigid semi-circular bladc attached to a long handle.

edging n

1 any of several materials used to form the edge of a lawn and prevent grass growing into flower beds and borders. Nowadays, edging is usually a thin strip of metal or plastic, sunk into the ground so that a lawn mower can run over it easily. 2 any of various plants used to form the edge of a border. Dwarf hedging used to be popular as edging but nowadays small flowering plants are more commonly used.

eelworm n

a tiny round-bodied worm that lives freely in the soil and attacks a wide variety of plants. Since this is practically impossible to control, infested plants should be destroyed.

elliptic adj

(of a leaf or sepal) oval in shape.

emarginate adj

(of a leaf) having smooth margins.

emasculate vt

to remove the male reproductive organs (of a flower) to prevent SELF-POLLINATION and allow CROSS-POLLINATION by a selected plant.

embryo n

a young seed plant that usually comprises a rudimentary plant with developing stem (plumule), root (radicle) and leaves (cotyledons).

endemic adj

(of a plant species) belonging naturally to a particular country or region, and not introduced.

endosperm n
a tissue in seed plants that is formed within the seed and provides nutrition for the developing embryo.

entire adj
(of a leaf) having a continuous, unindented margin.

ephemeral adj
(of a plant) having a very brief life or life cycle.

epicalyx n
a ring of BRACTS lying outside and usually resembling the CALYX of some flowers (eg those of potentillas).

epidermis n
the thin protective outer surface layer on plant organs.

epiphyte n
a plant that grows on another plant but derives its moisture and nutrients from the air and rain, eg lichens, mosses, and many types of ORCHIDS and BROMELIADS.

Epsom salts n
see SULPHATE OF MAGNESIUM.

ericaceous adj
of or being a member of the heather family that includes heathers and rhododendrons. Such plants hate lime and must be grown in ACID soils.

espalier n
1 a fruit tree or shrub trained to grow flat against a trellis or wires. **2** a support of upright posts and wires on which fruit trees can be trained.

etiolated adj
(of a plant) lanky and pallid from lack of light.

[1]**evergreen** adj
(of a tree or shrub) having leaves that remain green and functional throughout the year. Compare DECIDUOUS.

[2]**evergreen** n
a tree or shrub of this type.

everlasting adj
(of a plant) retaining its form or colour for a long time when dried, eg various members of the daisy family. Such a plant is known as an everlasting or an IMMORTELLE.

exhibition adj
(of a flower) highly developed for showing purposes, eg a dahlia or rose. Many exhibition varieties are unsuitable for outside exposure.

exotic adj
(of a plant) not native to the place where found.

exserted adj
(of a plant organ) projecting beyond the rest of the flower, eg PISTIL, STAMEN.

exstipulate adj
(of a plant organ) having no STIPULES.

extension shoot n
see LEADER.

[1]**eye** n
1 a flower centre, particularly one that is coloured or marked differently from the petals. **2** a single dormant bud growth, eg as found on a potato or dahlia TUBER. **3** a bud on some tomentose plants, eg grapevine, particularly when the stems have

been cut into single EYE CUTTINGS for propagation purposes.

eye cutting n

a short, HARDWOOD CUTTING taken during the DORMANT period and used to propagate plants such as grapevines and camellias. The cutting should be about 1.5 in (4 cm) long with a single growth bud or eye. A thin strip of bark is removed on the opposite side from the eye and the cutting pushed down into a sandy rooting medium so that the eye is just at soil level.

F_1 hybrid n

a first-generation plant arising from the CROSS-POLLINATION of two distinct pure-bred varieties. Seeds from F_1 hybrids are not necessarily identical to the parent plant, and cross-pollination must be repeated to reproduce the original HYBRID. They are usually very vigorous.

F_2 hybrid n

a second-generation plant arising from a CROSS-POLLINATION of two F_1 hybrids.

falcate adj

(of a leaf) hooked or curved like a sickle.

falls n

the outer petals of an iris which curve outward and in some species hang vertically.

family n

the category in the CLASSIFICATION of plants ranking above GENUS. A family consists of a number of related genera. eg, the Crassulaceae family includes *Sedum* and *Sempervivum* (houseleek); the Compositae family includes composite plants such as *Bellis* (daisy) and *Catananche* (Cupid's dart).

family tree n

an apple or pear tree which has three compatible

varieties grafted on a single ROOTSTOCK.

fan n

a fruit tree that has been pruned and shaped so that its branches radiate like a fan.

fancy adj

(of a flower) bred specially for its VARIEGATED blooms, eg EXHIBITION carnations.

farina n

a waxy powdery substance sometimes found on plant organs. Also **farinose** adj.

farmyard manure n

a manure made by mixing animal droppings with straw or litter. This is the type of manure usually used in the garden. The quality of any farmyard manure depends on the kind of animal that has produced it, the animal's diet, its bedding, and the length of time for which the manure has been stacked. Stable or horse manure is probably the best and is very good for heavy soils. Pig and cow manure, when well rotted, are very good on light soils. Farmyard manure is applied by being forked into the topsoil at the rate of a bucketful per square yard (square metre), or by being placed in 2 in (5 cm) layers at the bottom of trenches during autumn digging. It is often referred to by the abbreviation FYM.

fasciation n

a malformation of plant stems commonly manifested as an enlargement and flattening, as if several stems were fused. This condition may be found on a wide range of flowers, including delphiniums and lilies.

fascicle n
a small bundle or tuft. The term is used to refer to leaves, stems, roots or flowers (as in the flowerhead of sweet william).

fastigiate adj
(of a tree or shrub) having erect branches almost parallel with the tree trunk, eg the Lombardy poplar and the Irish yew.

feather n
a side shoot produced on the current year's growth of a MAIDEN tree.

feathered adj
1 *(of a young tree)* retaining the feathers growing on its main stem. **2** see BROKEN.

feather-veined adj
(of a leaf) having veins that spring up from the MIDRIB, giving the effect of a bird's feather.

feathery adj
see PLUMOSE.

felted adj
(of a plant part) covered with a dense growth of short hairs, eg the undersides of rhododendron leaves.

female adj
(of a plant or flower) having ovaries but no male reproductive parts. The male counterparts may appear on the same plant (as in the hazel tree) or on separate plants (as in the holly tree).

female flower n
a flower bearing only the female reproductive organs. See also PISTIL.

fermenting manure n
MANURE that is in the process of being broken down by a chemical reaction. Manure has to ferment before it is ready for use.

fern n
any of a class of flowerless, seedless plants which reproduce by means of spores carried on the undersides of their fronds.

fertile adj
1 *(of a plant)* producing abundantly. 2 *(of soil)* yielding good crops.

fertilization n
an act or process of POLLINATION.

fertilize vt
to apply a fertilizer to (soil).

fertilizer n
1 loosely, any substance (eg a manure or a chemical mixture) added to soil to provide nutrients for plants. 2 a substance other than bulky organic manure which provides plant nutrients in a relatively concentrated form. A 'straight' fertilizer supplies only one of the three major nutrients—NITROGEN, POTASSIUM, or PHOSPHORUS—which are essential to plant survival. A compound fertilizer, by contrast, provides all three nutrients, sometimes with the addition of other elements such as MANGANESE, MAGNESIUM, or IRON.

Fertilizers can be of ORGANIC or INORGANIC origin, and can come from a natural source or be manufactured. There is no difference in quality between organic and inorganic varieties, but the former is generally longer-lasting because the elements have to break down before they become available to the plant.

Fertilizers can be applied to the soil as a BASE DRESSING or as a TOP DRESSING, and it is unwise to use more than the quantity recommended as too much fertilizer can cause scorching of plant roots. Care should be taken to prevent the fertilizer from falling on foliage.

Concentrated fertilizers should generally be mixed with bulky organic materials such as peat or manure before use.

Commonly used fertilizers in the garden are BONEMEAL (providing phosphorus); DRIED BLOOD and HOOF AND HORN (supplying nitrogen); and SULPHATE OF POTASH (providing potassium).

fescue n

any of a genus *(Festuca)* of tufted grasses.

festoon vt

to train (a fruit tree) by bending its leader over in an arch and tying it to the stem when it is a maiden, and repeating the process in following years on vigorous shoots which have formed. Festooning keeps the tree small and encourages early fruiting.

fibrous adj

1 *(of a plant)* having a mass of fine roots, as distinguished from fewer fleshy roots. **2** *(of loam)* containing numerous fine roots, ie from rotted plants. Such loam is good for making soil-based potting composts.

filament n
the ANTHER-bearing stalk of a STAMEN.
filiform adj
(of a leaf) shaped like a filament; threadlike.
fillis n
a special soft string used for tying plants to supports.
fimbriate adj
(of a plant part) having fringed margins.
finger and toe n
see CLUB ROOT.
fire n
broadly, any disease that makes plant foliage look scorched. The term is used of specific plants, eg tulip fire.
fireblight n
a destructive and highly infectious bacterial disease affecting trees and shrubs of the rose family, including apples and pears. The leaves of infected shoots appear scorched or blackened.
firm vt
to press down and compact the soil or potting mixture around (a plant).
firmer n
a tool, usually a flat piece of wood with a handle, used for pushing down compost in seed boxes and pots to make it compact, smooth, and even.
flaked adj
see BROKEN.
flame gun n
a paraffin-burning torch that emits a long, intensely hot flame and is used to eliminate weeds

and burn garden debris.

flea beetle n

any of various small jumping beetles that attack the seedlings of cabbage, wallflower and related plants, and that sometimes carry virus diseases.

fleshy-rooted adj

(of a plant) having thick fleshy roots, or fleshy storage organs, eg a BULB or TUBER.

flore-pleno n

a plant having DOUBLE flowers.

floret n

a small flower, especially any of those forming a densely clustered flowerhead, eg in the daisy or dandelion.

floribunda n

any of various cultivated hybrid roses which bear large open clusters of flowers. See also HYBRID TEA.

floriferous adj

blooming freely.

[1]**flower** n

1 a blossom. **2** a shoot of a flowering plant that is specialized for reproduction and consists of a short axis bearing leaves modified to form PETALS, SEPALS, CARPELS and/or STAMENS. **3** a flowering plant.

[2]**flower** vi

to produce flowers; to blossom.

flowerbed n

a prepared bed, especially one used for cultivation of ornamental flowering plants.

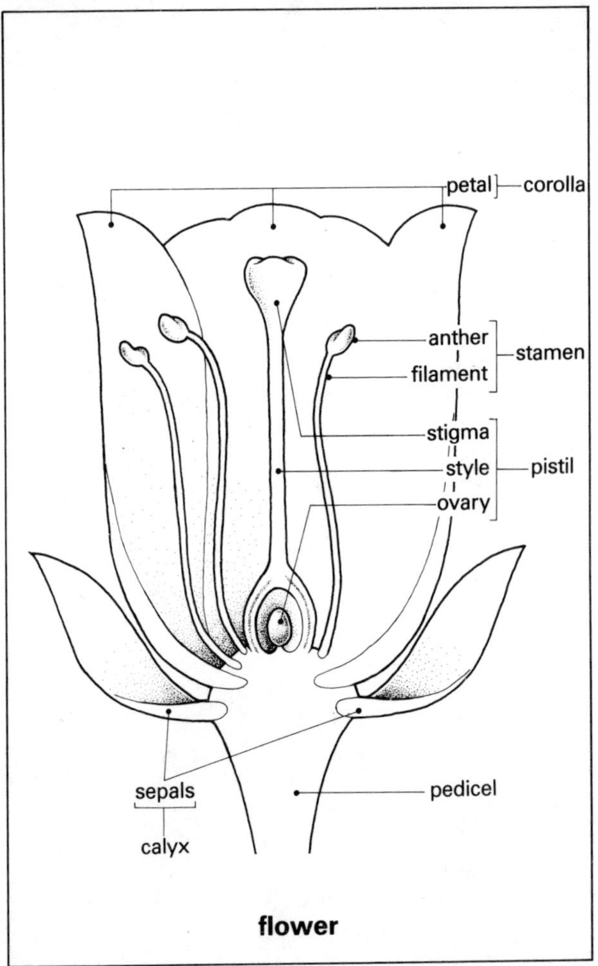
petal
corolla
anther
stamen
filament
stigma
style
pistil
ovary
sepals
calyx
pedicel

flower

flower bud n
a plant bud that produces only a flower.
flower-gatherer n
special SECATEURS designed to hold a flower after cutting it.
flowerhead n
an INFLORESCENCE composed of a rounded or flattened cluster of densely packed stalkless flowers arranged to look like a single flower.
flowering plant n
1 a plant that produces flowers, fruit and seed; an ANGIOSPERM. **2** a plant notable for, or cultivated for, its ornamental flowers.
flowerpot n
a container, typically the shape of a small bucket and with drainage holes in the base, in which to grow plants.
flower-spike n
a cylindrically-shaped FLOWERHEAD.
fluid sow vt
to sow (seeds) after mixing them with a gel or paste. Seeds sown this way are always germinated indoors; the fluid is squeezed out of a dispenser into prepared seed drills. This technique is supposed to speed up GERMINATION. Also known as liquid sow.
flush n
a sudden burst of plant growth, such as occurs with mushrooms or roses.
foliage n
1 the leaves of a plant or of a clump of plants. **2** a cluster of leaves, flowers and branches.

foliage leaf n
an ordinary green leaf, as distinguished from a PETAL, SCALE or similar modified or specialized leaf.

foliage plant n
a plant grown primarily for its decorative foliage.

foliar feed n
any of various fertilizers that can be applied to and absorbed by the leaves of a plant.

follicle n
a dry fruit consisting of one compartment containing many seeds and splitting open along one line when ripe, eg that of the delphinium. Compare CARPEL.

foot rot n
a plant disease marked by rotting of the stem near the ground. This is similar to DAMPING-OFFbut usually occurs at a later stage of growth. The disease can be controlled with BORDEAUX MIXTURE.

force vt
to induce (a plant) to produce flowers, fruit or vegetables early. This can be done by placing the plant in darkness and applying heat. The technique is used with plants grown for indoor decoration during the winter, or for early crops of rhubarb, seakale, etc.

fork n
1 a garden tool used for digging soil, consisting of two or more prongs set on the end of a handle.
2 the point on a tree at which two branches of similar age are joined. Compare CROTCH. **3** to dig

or work with a fork.

fork hoe n

see CANTERBURY HOE.

fork in vt

to dig or work (any material, eg manure) into soil with a fork.

form n

a botanical term for a naturally occurring VARIETY.

formal adj

(of a garden or border) having a mainly symmetrical or geometrical design and arrangement of plants.

formalin n

a strong disinfectant containing 40 per cent formaldehyde used for sterilizing greenhouse soil. This should be heavily diluted (49 parts water to 1 of formalin) and poured liberally on the soil. Watering should be repeated one week later. Plants should not be moved into the greenhouse until the fumes have completely dispersed. Formalin was once used for sterilizing seed boxes, pots and canes, but modern sterilants have replaced it in these uses.

frame n

a low-built structure covered with removable transparent material, usually glass or plastic, used for protecting plants growing outdoors. A garden frame can be used for many different purposes: to provide space when the greenhouse is overcrowded; to hasten seed GERMINATION; to obtain certain crops early, eg salad greens; to

HARDEN OFF tender plants raised in the greenhouse; to protect slightly tender plants in winter. Typically a frame is unheated but it can be heated with BOTTOM HEAT or heating cables around the sides.

frameworking n
the method of grafting parts of another variety of tree onto (a tree). The main branches are headed back and the side branches removed. SCIONS of the new variety, each with about six buds, are inserted every 8 to 10 inches (20 to 25 cm) along the branches. The tree should produce a crop again within two or three years.

friable adj
(of a soil) crumbly and easily worked.

froghopper n
any of numerous leaping garden insects whose larvae secrete froth. See also CUCKOO-SPIT INSECT.

frond n
1 a leaf, especially of a palm or fern. **2** a leaf-like plant body of a FUNGUS, LICHEN or similar plant.

frost n
1 the temperature that causes freezing, ie 0°C, 32°F. See also AIR FROST and GROUND FROST. **2** a covering of minute ice crystals on a cold surface.

[1]**fruit** n
1 the seed-bearing part of any plant. **2** an edible growth formed by the seed-bearing part of a plant, especially a sweet or fleshy pulp associated with

the seed. See also BERRY, DRUPE.

[2]fruit vi

to produce or bear fruit.

fruit bud n

a bud on the branch of a fruit tree from which leaves, flowers and fruit will grow.

fruiting body n

the reproductive (ie spore-producing) organ of a large FUNGUS, eg mushroom or toadstool.

fumigant n

a substance used in fumigating.

fumigate vt

to expose (an enclosed area, eg a greenhouse) to poisonous fumes in order to destroy insects, pests or fungus growths.

fungicidal paint n

any FUNGICIDE in paint form, used to treat diseased or wounded plants.

fungicide n

any chemical that kills a fungus and/or inhibits its growth. Fungicides can be ORGANIC or INORGANIC in origin and come in liquid, powder or smoke form. Some fungicides, eg CAPTAN, can be used as seed dressings to prevent fungus disease.

fungus n, pl **fungi**

any of a major group (*Fungi*) of organisms that lack the green pigment CHLOROPHYLL, are parasitic and feed on dead or decaying plants. Many fungi cause a variety of plant disease and must be controlled with appropriate fungicides.

fusiform adj
(of a plant part) tapering towards each end.

FYM abb
see FARMYARD MANURE.

gall n
a diseased swelling of plant tissues owing to fungus or to infection by insect parasites. This may be found on the roots, stems, leaves or flowers of a plant; it may slow plant growth but rarely causes serious damage.

gamete n
the sexual cell (eg POLLEN or OVULE) in a plant capable of fusing with another in reproduction.

gamma-BHC n
see HCH.

gamopetalous adj
(of a flower) having petals that are united to form a cup or tube, eg in the primrose or petunia.

garden line n
a length of cord with a spike at each end used for marking out straight lines in a garden, especially for hoeing or making seed drills. Also known as a hoeing line.

gene n
a unit of inheritance, carried on a CHROMOSOME.

genus n, pl **genera**
a unit of plant CLASSIFICATION. Plants with

similar botanical characteristics are placed together in a genus. Thus all buttercup-shaped flowers, for example, are placed together in the genus *Ranunculus*. A plant's genus is indicated by its first botanical name, which is usually written with an initial capital letter.

germinate vi
(of a seed) to begin to grow or sprout.

germination n
the beginning of growth or sprouting in a seed.

glabrous adj
(of a plant organ) having a smooth hairless surface.

gland n
any of various secreting organs of plants.

glasshouse n
see GREENHOUSE.

glaucous adj
(of a plant) having a dull blue or blue-grey colour.

globose adj
(of a plant organ) shaped like a globe, spherical. The term is often applied to plant fruits.

glochid n
a small barbed hair, characteristic of many types of CACTUS.

glyphosate n
a systemic weedkiller that has a slow but powerful effect, travelling through a plant to kill off all its parts both above and below ground. It is available in either liquid or gel form.

[1]**graft** vt
to unite the stem or bud of (a plant) with the root

of another plant. This is done either to form another individual plant or to implant the characteristics of the rootstock. The stem or bud (scion) is cut and either inserted in the tissue of the rootstock or aligned with a corresponding cut and the two cut sections are bound together and sealed with a waxy compound until the plant tissues unite.

²graft n

1 the union of a plant SCION with the ROOTSTOCK of another plant. **2** the particular technique used to cause a union between plant tissues. See also APPROACH GRAFT, BARK GRAFT, BOTTLE GRAFT, BRIDGE GRAFT, CLEFT GRAFT, CROWN GRAFT, OBLIQUE SIDE GRAFT, SADDLE GRAFT, SIDE GRAFT, SPLICE GRAFT, STUB GRAFT, WHIP AND TONGUE GRAFT. **3** a plant resulting from a graft or process of grafting.

³graft n

see GRAFTING TOOL.

grafting n

a method of PROPAGATION in which plant parts from two different but related plants are caused to unite and grow together. This is a complicated process and there are many techniques used in producing fruit trees and roses. See GRAFT. See also FRAMEWORKING, TOPWORKING.

grafting knife n

a special knife used in making a GRAFT. This has a 3 in (7.5 cm) blade with an angled point, and a longer handle of about 5 in (12.5 cm).

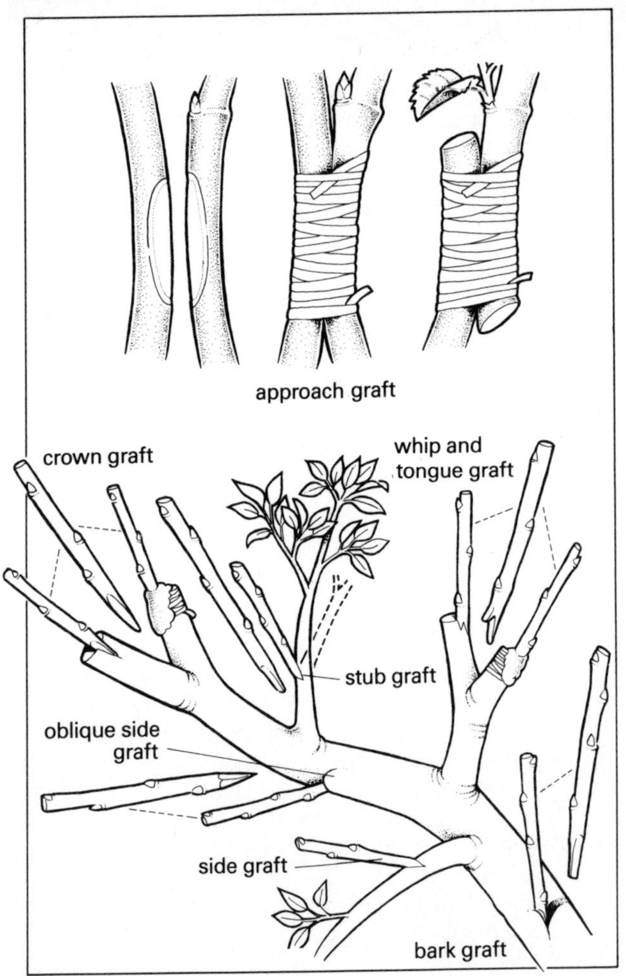
approach graft
crown graft
whip and tongue graft
stub graft
oblique side graft
side graft
bark graft

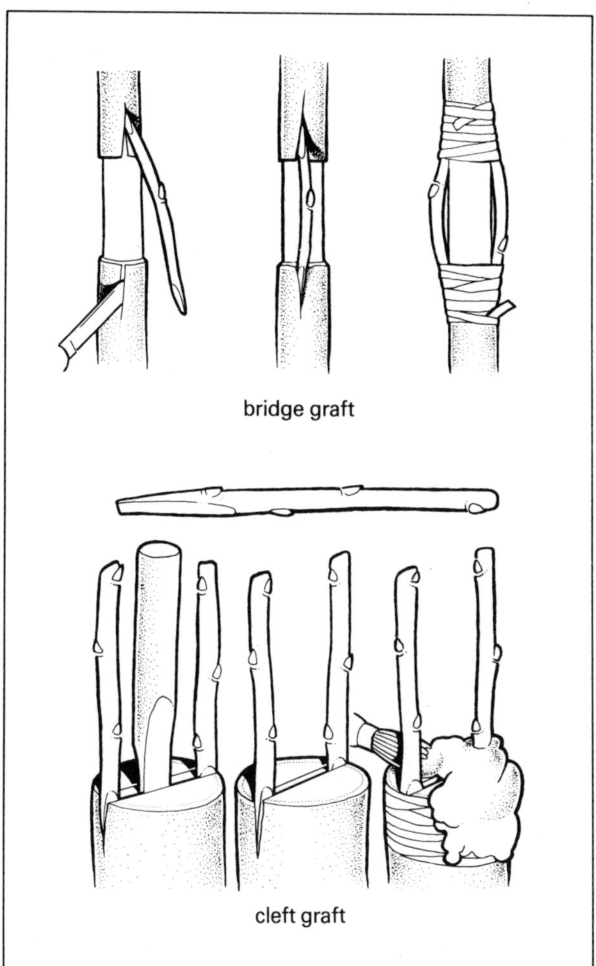

bridge graft

cleft graft

grafting tool n
a special spade with a concave blade used for digging a drainage trench. Also called GRAFT.

grafting wax n
a substance used to cover and protect the wounded surface of a GRAFT.

grass n
any of a large family (*Gramineae*, the grass family) of monocotyledonous, mostly non-woody plants having jointed stems sheathed by slender leaves and bearing tiny flowers in spikelets.

grass down vt
to sow grass around the base of (a fruit tree). This slows down growth and encourages fruiting more effectively than leaving the area bare.

gravel n
a substance consisting of loose rounded fragments of rock, usually mixed with sand. It has numerous uses in the garden, including as a cover for greenhouse STAGING and to improve drainage in ALPINE GARDENS.

grease-band n
a sticky band of petroleum jelly or a special fruit-tree grease applied in the autumn to the trunk or main branch of a fruit tree at least 18in (45cm) above ground level. The band traps any insect crawling up the tree to lay eggs in the branches or twigs.

Grecian saw n
a narrow-bladed curved saw used for cutting out small tree branches.

green-cluster adj
(of a bud stage) referring to the stage in fruit-bud development after that of BUD-BURST, when the bud scales drop off and a tight cluster of green flower buds can be seen in each leaf rosette.

greenfly n, pl **greenflies, greenfly**
any of various green-coloured APHIDS that are frequently carriers of plant VIRUS DISEASE and are destructive to plants.

greenhouse n
an enclosure with a transparent glass or plastic roof and walls used for the cultivation or protection of tender plants and seedlings.

There are several different types of greenhouse available, usually with wood or aluminium frames. The four main shapes are: free-standing span roof, which is often clad with timber up to the level of the STAGING; the Dutch light, with sloping sides and glass panels reaching the ground on all sides; lean-to greenhouses, which lean against one wall of a house or garden wall; and circular greenhouses, which are economical on space and easy to work in.

Whatever its shape or size, a greenhouse should have good ventilation and a regular and plentiful supply of water. It will probably also need some form of shading, such as slatted blinds, to protect plants from direct sunlight in hot weather. Unless it is to be a COLD HOUSE, it will also need some form of heating, though in much of Britain, artificial heat is needed for only about one third of the year. Gas, paraffin and electric heaters are

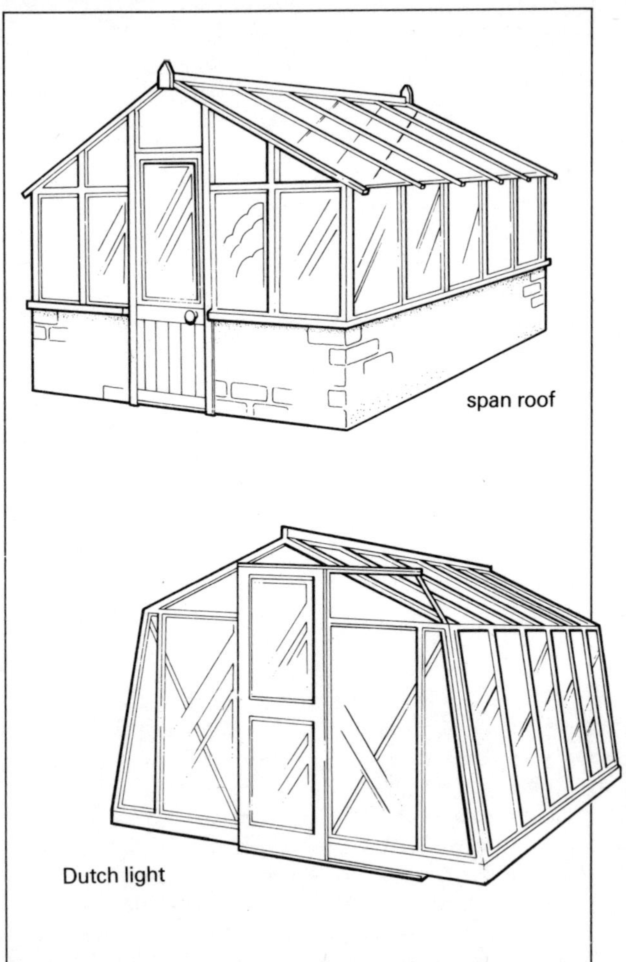
span roof
Dutch light

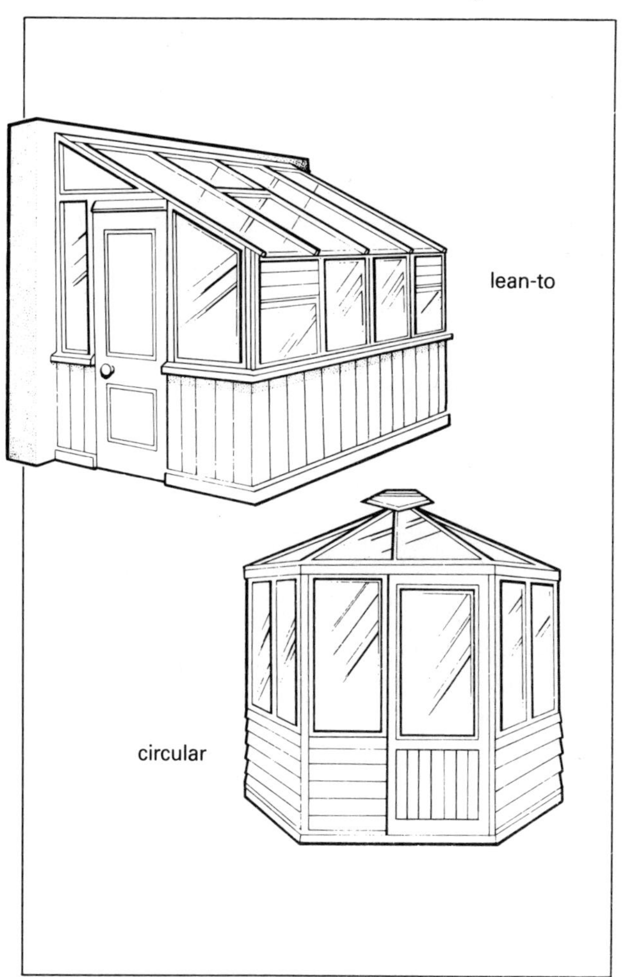
lean-to
circular

available and heating systems vary greatly in their range and sophistication.

A greenhouse must be kept clean to prevent plant disease, and it is necessary to FUMIGATE the interior at the end of each growing season. Also known as a glasshouse.

[1]green manure n

a rapidly-growing plant crop, eg mustard or rape, dug into the soil as enrichment while it is still green. Also called cover crop.

[2]green manure vt

to enrich (soil) by digging in green manure.

ground-cover plant n

any of various low-growing plants used to cover the soil under trees or between bushes. These usually provide a weed-proof cover of leaves requiring little or no maintenance.

ground frost n

a temperature below freezing on the ground, harmful to low-growing vegetation.

groundwork n

the lower plants in a bedding scheme composed of plants of different heights.

growing bag n

a large plastic bag filled with peat-based potting compost in which a variety of plants can be grown. It provides the plants' roots with as much nourishment and room to grow as they need. It is ideal for a small balcony where there is no soil or where garden soil is unsuitable for certain plants.

growing board n

a lightweight board made of dehydrated potting

compost and surrounded by a plastic bag. Soaked in water, the board expands into a full-sized growing bag.

growing medium n
any substance in which a plant can grow and flourish.

growing point n
the part of a shoot or branch from which extension growth occurs.

Growmore n
a standardized general-purpose compound fertilizer, originally formulated by the Ministry of Agriculture, which contains roughly equal amounts of PHOSPHORUS, NITROGEN and POTASSIUM.

growth bud n
a bud from which a shoot or leaf will grow.

growth substance n
any of various hormonal preparations that affect the growth of plants. They are available in liquid or powder form and are used to root CUTTINGS, suppress weeds, and set fruit.

gum vi
(of a plant) to exude a substance, especially gum resin. This usually occurs in response to a wound, for which the gum provides a protective covering. Trees that gum without being wounded are probably in bad health.

gummosis n
1 the abnormal production of gum resin by a plant owing to disease. **2** a plant disease characterized by gummosis.

guttation n
the oozing of water or watery fluid from an uninjured plant surface, eg through specialized pores in the outer layer of leaves, stems, etc. In houseplants this is an indication that the potting compost is too wet.

guy vt
to support (a tree) by means of wires fastened to pegs in the ground. Three wires are fixed fairly high up on the trunk and then fastened to the pegs, which should be hammered into the ground at equal spacings.

gymnosperm n
any of a class or subdivision of woody seed-bearing plants (eg conifers and yews) having their seeds not enclosed in an OVARY. Compare ANGIOSPERM.

gynandrous adj
(of a flower) having the male and female parts united in a column. Some orchids are gynandrous.

gynoecium n
all the female parts of a flower.

habit n
the characteristic mode of growth of a plant.

half-hardy adj
(of a plant) able to withstand moderately low temperatures but injured by frost.

half-moon n
see EDGER.

half-ripe adj
(of a stem cutting) taken from the parent plant in the late summer and from the current year's wood.

half-ripe cutting n
a STEM CUTTING prepared from a firm side shoot of current year's wood, taken during June, July or August. Most shrubs are propagated by such cuttings.

half-standard adj
(of a plant, tree or shrub) resembling a standard in form, but with a shorter length of bare stem.

half trench vt
see DOUBLE DIG.

hand fork n
a short-handled fork used for working close to the soil.

harden off vt
to cause (a plant) to become accustomed to cold or other unfavourable environmental conditions. Plants that have been germinated and grown to seedling stage under cover are put outside for an increasing length of time each day.

hardpan n
see PAN.

hard prune vt
to cut (growing shoots) back to a point within a few dormant buds above ground. The most drastic form of pruning, this can reinvigorate an old root system into new growth and rejuvenate overgrown trees. See also PRUNE.

hardwood cutting n
a STEM CUTTING taken between October and February from a firm and ripened side shoot of current year's growth. Hardwood cuttings should be allowed to develop roots for a complete growing season before being lifted and planted in their permanent positions. Trees, hardy shrubs, and soft fruits are usually propagated by such cuttings.

hardy adj
(of a plant) able to withstand frost during a normal winter.

hastate adj
(of a leaf) shaped like the triangular head of a spear and heavily lobed at the base.

haulm n
the unproductive stems and tops of vegetable crop plants, eg potatoes, beans and peas, after they

have been harvested.

haw n

a hawthorn berry.

HCH abb

a refined form of the synthetic insecticide BHC (benzene hexachloride), also known as gamma-BHC. This is very effective against most garden pests and is available in dust, spray, and smoke forms. It should not be used on certain plants, eg cucumbers, vines, hydrangeas, or beetroots, and crops sprayed with it should not be harvested for at least two weeks after application. HCH used to be known as lindane.

head n

1 a cluster of flowers crowded at the end of a stalk, as in the hyacinth. **2** the branch system of a STANDARD or HALF-STANDARD tree. **3** a mature lettuce, cauliflower or cabbage.

head back vt

to PRUNE (trees or shrubs) by cutting back some or all of the branches above well-developed dormant buds. The term is usually applied to the cutting back of fruit trees. Also known as head down.

head down vt

see HEAD BACK.

heading n

see HEARTING.

hearting n

the stage at which a leaf vegetable, eg a cabbage, first produces its tight head of growth. Also called heading.

heading back

heart rot n
the process or result of decaying in a plant's internal tissues.

heart-wood n
the older, harder, non-living wood in the centre of the trunk or main branch of a tree.

heave vi
1 *(of soil)* to rise up, eg as a result of the action of frost on damp soil. 2 *(of plants or roots)* to rise or become uprooted, eg as a result of the freezing and thawing of soil.

hedge trimmer n
a power- or hand-operated tool used to keep formal hedges neatly shaped. Powered trimmers can be run on electricity (mains or batteries) or on petrol, and various attachments are available for different types of hedge.

heel n
a small piece of bark left on the bottom of a side shoot when it is pulled from a plant for the purpose of PROPAGATION.

heel cutting n
any STEM CUTTING pulled away from the main shoot with a small strip of bark (heel) attached. The edges of the heel should be trimmed before being inserted into the soil. In some cases, cuttings with heels STRIKE more easily than those cut cleanly below a NODE.

heel-in vt
to plant (cuttings or plants) temporarily before setting in the final growing position. Plants can remain in good condition for several weeks.

hen-and-chickens n
any of several plants (eg the houseleek) that multiply by producing offsets from the base of the parent plant.

hep n
see HIP.

herb n
1 a seed-producing plant that does not develop persistent woody tissue but dies down at the end of a growing season. See also HERBACEOUS. **2** a plant (eg parsley, thyme or mint) or plant part valued for its medicinal, savoury or aromatic qualities.

herbaceous adj
1 *(of a plant)* of, being or having the characteristics of a herb. Strictly, the term applies to ANNUAL, BIENNIAL and PERENNIAL plants, but it is usually loosely applied to perennials that die down in the winter and reappear the following spring. **2** *(of a plant stem)* having little or no woody tissue and persisting usually only for a single growing season. **3** *(of a petal or sepal)* having the colour, texture, or appearance of a leaf.

herbaceous border n
a permanent flower border of herbaceous plants.

herb garden n
a garden or part of a garden in which herbs are cultivated.

herbicide n
a chemical used to destroy or inhibit plant

growth; broadly, a weedkiller.

hermaphrodite n

a plant with both male and female reproductive organs.

heterophyllous adj

(of a plant) bearing leaves of different shape at different times of its life, as in the juvenile and adult leaves of the eucalyptus.

hill-up vt

see EARTH-UP.

hip n

the ripened fruit of a rose. Also called hep.

hirsute adj

(of a plant part) covered with coarse, stiff hairs.

hispid adj

(of a plant part) rough or covered with bristles, stiff hairs or minute spines.

hoary adj

(of a plant part) having greyish or whitish hairs.

[1]**hoe** n

any of various instruments, usually with a long wooden handle and a flat blade, used principally to AERATE the soil and destroy weeds. See CANTERBURY HOE, DRAW HOE, DUTCH HOE.

[2]**hoe** vt

to work (soil) with a hoe.

hoeing line n

see GARDEN LINE.

honeydew n

a sugary substance deposited on the leaves of plants, usually by APHIDS or SCALE INSECTS and sometimes by FUNGUS.

honey fungus n
scientifically known as *Armillaria mellea,* a soil-borne disease that attacks tree roots and eventually the trunk of the tree. Yellow and brown growths resembling mushrooms near the tree's base are often the first symptom. There is no cure, so affected trees should be removed.

hooded adj
(of a plant part) shaped like a hood, eg the flower of the gladiolus, whose petal tips curve inwards.

hoof and horn n
an organic fertilizer used to supply NITROGEN to the soil. This is slow-acting and long-lasting.

hop manure n
a manure comprising dry spent hops to which have been added chemical plant foods such as SULPHATE OF AMMONIA and SULPHATE OF POTASH. Hop manure is best applied in the spring, and the manufacturer's instructions should be followed carefully.

hormone n
1 a natural substance which circulates in the sap of plants and regulates growth, bud and root formation. **2** a synthetic substance that acts like a natural plant hormone.

hormone rooting powder n
see ROOTING POWDER.

horse manure n
a farmyard manure made from horse droppings and stable litter. One of the most valuable types of farmyard manure, this is fibrous, absorbent, relatively dry and easy to handle. It is best for

clay soils and is excellent as a fermenting manure for making a HOTBED.

hose n

a flexible tube for conveying water to the garden. Rubber hoses are still available but plastic hoses are more common, as they are tougher and longer-lasting. Perforated hoses for distributing water along rows of vegetables are also available.

hose-in-hose n

an abnormal floral arrangement in which the flowers seem to grow in pairs, one out of the centre of another. This mutation is found in certain flowers such as primrose and polyanthus. A wide variety of hose-in-hose flowers are cultivated.

host plant n

any plant on which a parasite lives.

hotbed n

a bed of soil enclosed in glass, heated especially by fermenting manure, and used to force plants or raise seedlings. See also BOTTOM HEAT.

hothouse n

a heated greenhouse, especially one in which tropical plants can be grown.

houseplant n

any plant grown or kept indoors.

hover mower n

a lawn mower, run by electricity or a petrol engine, that is supported on a cushion of air provided by fans. A hover mower can move easily in any direction and over bumpy ground.

humidity n
(the degree of) moisture, especially in the atmosphere.

humus n
a brown or black material that results from partial decomposition of plant or animal matter and forms the fertile ORGANIC portion of the soil.

hybrid n
a plant deriving from the crossing of two different species, either in the same genus or from different genera. Also known as cross. See also CLASSIFICATION; F_1 HYBRID; F_2 HYBRID; TRUE-BREEDING.

hybridize vi
to produce HYBRIDS; to interbreed. This is done by taking POLLEN from a male plant and mixing it with the STIGMA of the female plant.

hybrid tea n
any of various cultivated hybrid roses which usually flower continuously throughout the summer and have double flowers which are borne singly or in a small group on each stem. The traditional distinction between a hybrid tea and a FLORIBUNDA has been eroded by recent interbreeding; a new classification devised by the Royal National Rose Society replaces the two terms by *large-flowered* and *cluster-flowered.*

hybrid vigour n
the quality of many hybrids that causes them to grow bigger or produce more flowers or fruit than their parents. Hybrid vigour declines with each

generation so the original cross must be made each year.

hydrophyte n

a plant that grows on or in waterlogged soil.

hydroponics n

the growing of plants in dilute nutrient solutions without soil. See SOILLESS CULTURE.

imbricate adj
(of a bract, leaf or scale arrangement) having or being in an overlapping, regularly ordered arrangement, eg the rosettes of the houseleek and the scales on the bud of a horse chestnut.

immortelle n
see EVERLASTING.

immune adj
(of a plant) having a high degree of resistance to certain pests and diseases.

inarch n
see APPROACH GRAFT.

incinerator n
a metal container used for burning any garden waste that cannot be rotted down on a COMPOST HEAP.

incised adj
(of a bract margin, leaf or stipule) deeply and sharply toothed.

incurved adj
(of a flower) having FLORETS which curve over and into the centre of the blossom to form a firm head. The term is mainly used of a certain group of chrysanthemums. Compare INTERMEDIATE, RECURVED, REFLEXED.

indeterminate adj
(of a plant) having a stem that grows indefinitely rather than ending in a flower bud or TRUSS, eg the tomato. Compare DETERMINATE.

inflorescence n
1 the (mode of) arrangement of flowers on a stem. Types include CAPITULUM, CORYMB, CYME, PANICLE, RACEME, SPADIX, SPIKE, UMBEL, WHORL. **2** a flower cluster. **3** the budding and unfolding of blossoms; flowering.

informal adj
(of a garden or border) having a mainly irregular design and arrangement of plants.

inorganic adj
(of a chemical compound) being or composed of matter other than plant or animal, and lacking carbon. The term is used especially of chemical fertilizers, eg SULPHATE OF AMMONIA.

insecticide n
any of various substances used for killing garden insects, available in liquid, powder, smoke or vapour forms.

insectivorous adj
(of a plant) feeding on insects.

intercrop n
a quick-growing crop grown between rows of slower-growing crops, eg radishes between rows of peas or lettuces between onions. Compare CATCH CROP.

intermediate adj
(of a flower) having blooms with florets that curve inward loosely and do not close tight on top. The

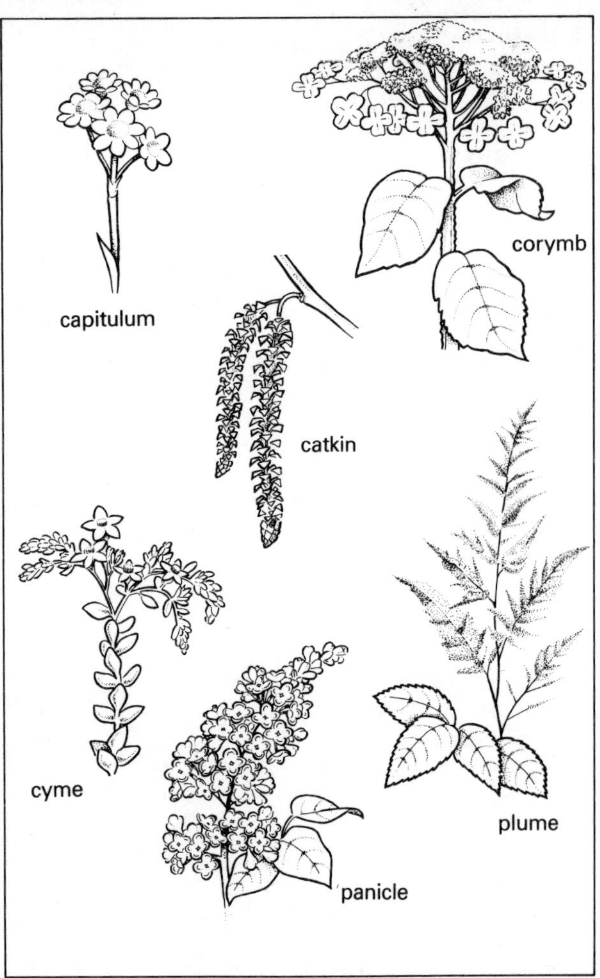
corymb
capitulum
catkin
cyme
plume
panicle

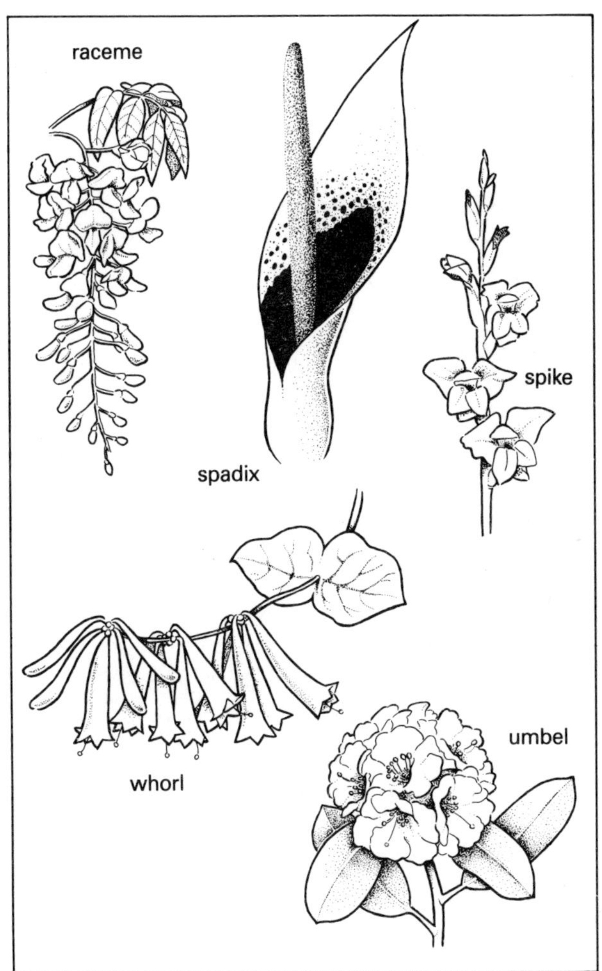
raceme
spadix
spike
whorl
umbel

term is used especially of chrysanthemums. Compare INCURVED, RECURVED, REFLEXED.

internodal cutting n

a STEM CUTTING of half-ripe wood cut halfway between two NODES, as opposed to just below a node. Clematis is often propagated with internodal cuttings.

internode n

the length of bare stem between NODES.

[1]**intersow** vi

to sow an INTERCROP.

[2]**intersow** vt

to sow (a row of plants etc) as an INTERCROP.

involucre n

a WHORL or BRACT or more than one, situated below and close to a flower or fruit, eg the basal sheathing leaves of a daisy.

Irishman's cutting n

a single shoot used for PROPAGATION which already has a few roots formed on it. Taken from the crown of a plant, this is really a small DIVISION rather than a true CUTTING. Early-growing chrysanthemums are sometimes propagated in this manner.

iron n

a naturally occurring mineral substance which is a TRACE ELEMENT essential for plant growth.

iron deficiency n

the lack of iron in the soil. A typical symptom in plants is CHLOROSIS, when leaves turn white or yellow. Iron deficiency can be a serious problem but it occurs only in soils with a high LIME content. It can be remedied by applications of a SEQUESTRENE.

irregular adj
(of a flower) unable to be cut into equal halves in any plane.

irrigate vt
to supply water to (soil, crops, etc) by artificial means.

island bed n
a flowerbed set off on its own, usually surrounded by a lawn and with tall plants planted in the centre, shorter plants around the edge.

John Innes compost n
a standardized potting compost developed at the John Innes Horticultural Institute. This can be bought ready-mixed or as ingredients for mixing, and there are three varieties. All contain seven parts medium sterilized LOAM, three parts PEAT and two parts coarse sand; they differ in the amount of fertilizer added. No. 1 contains, per bushel (36.3 l), 3/4 ounce (21.2 g) of ground limestone or chalk, and 4 ounces (113.4 g) of a base fertilizer made from two parts superphosphate of lime, two parts HOOF AND HORN meal, and one part SULPHATE OF POTASH. No. 2 has twice the amount of added fertilizer and No. 3 three times the amount. The strength of compost to use depends on the size of the plants requiring potting: Nos. 2 and 3 are suitable for stronger-growing plants. John Innes seed compost used for raising seedlings consists of two parts medium sterilized loam, one part peat and one part coarse sand. To each bushel is added $1\frac{1}{2}$ ounces (42.5 g) SUPERPHOSPHATE OF LIME and 3/4 ounce (21.2 g) of ground limestone or chalk.

joint n
see NODE.

June drop n
the falling of immature fruits on fruit trees during June and July. This is usually a natural way of balancing a large crop but may also be caused by external factors such as inadequate watering or by lack of vigour. Careful pruning and good watering can prevent unnecessary loss of fruit.

juvenile adj
(of plant growth or foliage) being in a distinct early stage which differs markedly from the adult stage; eg the leaves of the young eucalyptus are very different in shape from those of the mature plant; ivy produces juvenile climbing stems and PALMATE leaves, but has adult non-climbing stems and OVATE or LANCEOLATE leaves.

kainite n

a naturally-occurring chemical compound of sulphate of magnesium, potassium sulphate, magnesium chloride and common salt chemically combined with water and used as a fertilizer. Kainite is useful in adding POTASSIUM to the soil and should be applied in the autumn.

keel n

the two lower linked petals formed in the flowers of certain LEGUMINOUS plants, eg the lupin and garden pea. The petals are pressed together in the shape of a boat keel.

key n

the winged seed pod of the sycamore, lime or ash.

kitchen garden n

a garden or part of a garden in which vegetables are cultivated for use in cooking.

knife-ring vi

see BARK-RING.

knob n

the swollen point on the branch of a fruit tree where the previous year's fruit stalk was attached. Since this is where new fruit buds will develop, the knob should not be removed.

knock-down adj

(of a pesticide) fast-acting and not long-lasting.

label n
a small, flat, pointed stick used to identify a plant, usually made of plastic, wood, or metal. It is either attached to the plant or inserted into the soil beside it. Plastic and metal labels are more durable than wood and can be written upon with special inks.

labellum n
the large and distinctive middle petal of an orchid flower.

labiate adj
(of a plant) having petals or sepals arranged in two unequal portions that project one over the other like lips, eg the snapdragon.

laciniate adj
(of a leaf or petal) bordered by a fringe.

ladybird n
any of numerous small nearly hemispherical often brightly coloured beetles. The ladybird is the gardener's friend since the insect and its larvae feed on garden pests, eg APHIDS and currant MITES.

lamina n
the broad, flat part of a leaf, as distinct from its stem.

lanceolate adj
(of a leaf) tapering to a point at the tip and sometimes also at the base.

lanky adj
(of a stem) having a spindly and gaunt appearance.

larva n, pl **larvae**
an insect in the first stage of its life after emerging from the egg. Some larvae, eg those of the CHAFER BEETLE, can cause damage to garden plants.

latent adj
see DORMANT.

[1]**lateral** adj
(of a stem, bud or shoot) branching out from the side of the leader or from the main branch. This term is usually applied to fruit trees to explain where to prune. Generally, the lateral stems are the fruit producers and the leaders extend the branch system of the plant.

[2]**lateral** n
a stem, bud or shoot that produces fruit. Compare LEADER.

latex n
a milky or yellowish fluid that is produced by the cells of various flowering plants, eg of the spurge and poppy families.

lawn n
an area of ground usually covered with grass and kept mown. A lawn can be either grown from seed or laid with TURF. There are many types of grass seed available and choice of seed depends on the

type of lawn required, the soil of the site, and the amount of wear the lawn is likely to have. The main lawn grasses are FESCUES and BENT GRASSES, and perennial rye grasses and smooth-stalked meadow grasses. Fescues and bent grasses have narrow leaves, withstand mowing well and are usually used to create a very close, smooth turf. They need good drainage and aeration, but are not highly resistant to weed invasion. Rye grass and meadow grass are strong-growing and hard-wearing, and are the best grasses for a lawn that is to be used frequently by children.

Turf provides a usable lawn faster than seed but is much more expensive.

Lawns can also be sown with more unusual plants such as camomile or thyme, both of which have the added merit of being aromatic.

Established lawns should be cut regularly between March and October. They should be fed in the spring with a quick-acting lawn fertilizer and in the autumn with a slow-acting lawn fertilizer and TOP DRESSING. Lawns should be watered in dry weather, aerated when they become compacted, and raked to remove dead grass, debris and leaves. It is not necessary to roll an ordinary garden lawn.

lawn edger n

see EDGER.

lawn mower n

a machine for cutting the grass on a lawn. The two major types of domestic lawn mower are the cylinder, or reel, and the rotary cutter. Cylinder mowers can be either mechanical or power-operated and are used on lawns that need to be kept well mown. Side-wheel models are cheaper, but they cannot cut close to lawn edges; rear-roller models, in addition to cutting the grass, roll the lawn and collect the mowings in a grass box. Rotary mowers have high-speed rotary blades and can be of the wheeled or hover type. The latter is useful for cutting grass on slopes. Rotary mowers do not cut as close as cylinder mowers but they are much more effective on grass more than 3 in (7.5 cm) high. Power-operated mowers can be driven by petrol, mains electricity or battery.

lawn rake n

a rake designed especially for use on grass lawns. This is fan-shaped and made of wire, plastic or bamboo, and is useful for removing cut grass, leaves and other debris.

lawn sand n

a combination of sand and chemicals used for killing weeds and moss on lawns and for stimulating grass growth. This can be used in spring or summer but not in very hot weather, when it may encourage scorching of the grass.

[1]**layer** vt

to propagate (a plant) by inducing shoots to take root while still attached to and growing from the plant. A branch or shoot is bent downwards and pegged into the soil so that it can make roots. This is best done using half-ripened shoots and the buried part of the stem is partially severed and held in place with a stone or bent wire. When roots have formed, the original shoot is severed from the parent plant and may then be potted up or planted out. The best time to layer shrubs is in late spring or early summer; for soft-wooded plants summer is best.

[2]**layer** n

1 a branch or shoot of a plant treated in such a way as to induce it to take root while still attached to the parent plant. **2** a plant developed from a rooted layer.

layering n

a method or process used to layer a plant, usually artificially. There are also natural examples of layering, as in strawberry runners which produce new rooting plants, or forsythia which may root into the soil when a low-sweeping branch comes into contact with the ground. See also AIR LAYERING, SERPENTINE LAYERING, TIP LAYERING.

[1]**leach** vt

to remove soluble materials from (soil) by draining water through it.

[2]**leach** vi

(of soluble materials) to become removed from soil by draining.

leader n

the main or end shoot that extends a plant's existing branch system. Also called extension shoot. Compare LATERAL.

leaf n

any of the usually green, flat and typically broad-bladed outgrowths from the stem of a plant that

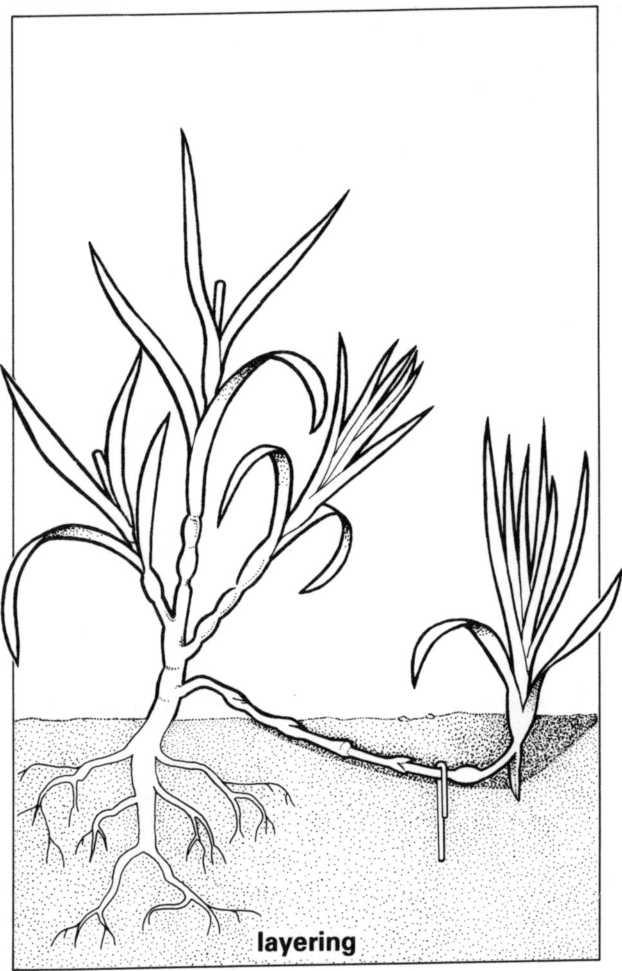
layering

function primarily in the manufacture of food for the plant by PHOTOSYNTHESIS. Leaves come in many shapes and sizes and have different arrangements on the plants' stems. They are one of the main identifying characteristics of a plant.

leaf beetle n

any of a family (*Chrysomelidae*) of numerous small brightly coloured leaf-eating beetles.

leaf blotch n

a plant disease caused by a fungus that attacks the leaves of cereals, especially barley, and adversely affects the development of the grain.

leaf bud n

a plant bud that develops into a leafy shoot and does not produce flowers.

leaf-bud cutting n

a STEM CUTTING of half-ripe wood with a leaf attached and a growth bud in the leaf axil. The cutting is taken during the summer and inserted in soil so that the leaf and bud are just above the surface. Camellias are often propagated by this method. Also known as bud cutting. Compare LEAF CUTTING.

leaf curl n

1 a fungal disease that causes the leaves of peaches, almonds and nectarines to curl and discolour. The affected leaves should be picked off and the plant sprayed with a fungicide. **2** any of various viral diseases characterized by a curling of leaves.

leaf cutter bee n

any of various bees that live alone rather than in

leaf arrangements

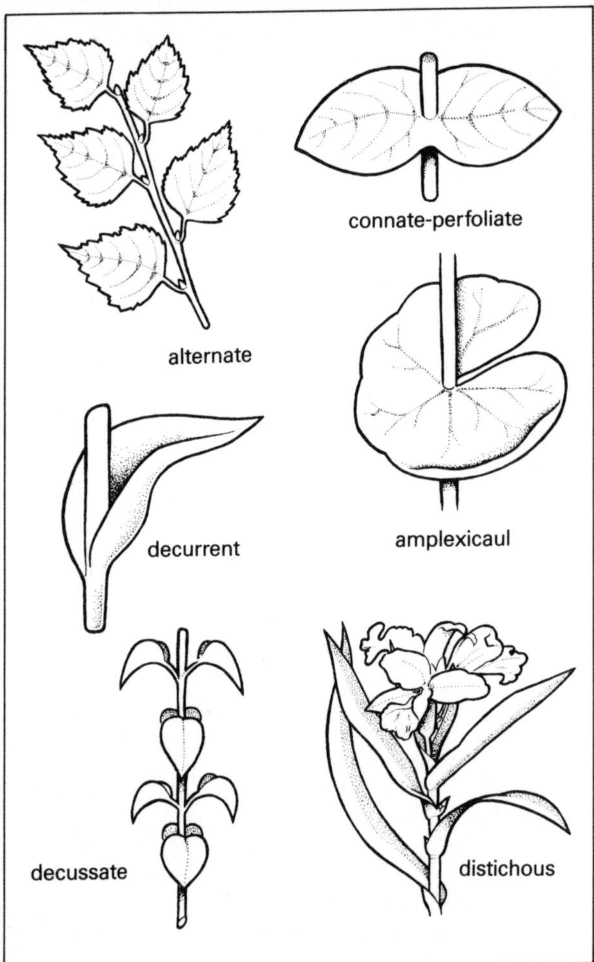

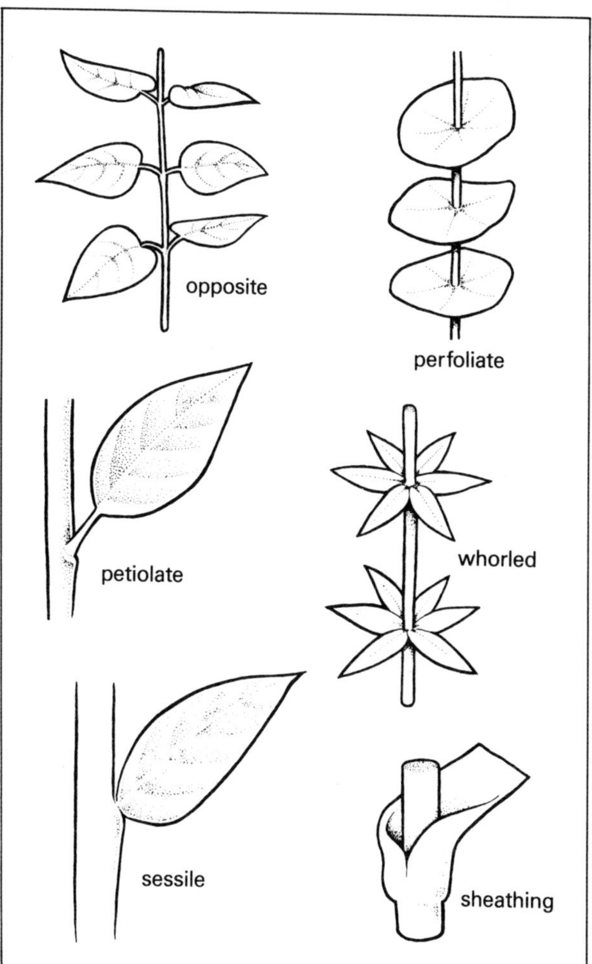
opposite
perfoliate
petiolate
whorled
sessile
sheathing

leaf shapes

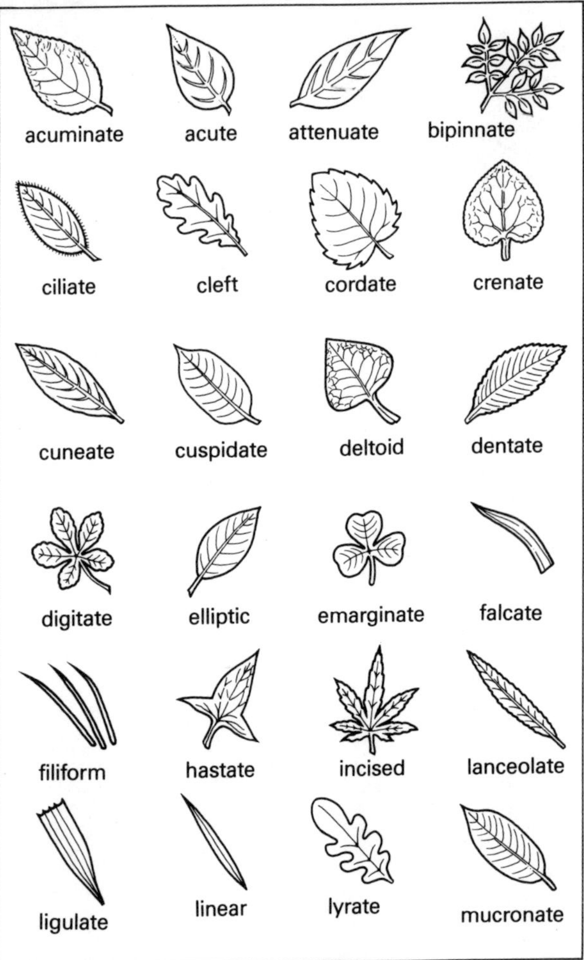
acuminate
acute
attenuate
bipinnate
ciliate
cleft
cordate
crenate
cuneate
cuspidate
deltoid
dentate
digitate
elliptic
emarginate
falcate
filiform
hastate
incised
lanceolate
ligulate
linear
lyrate
mucronate

oblanceolate
oblong
obtuse
obvate
orbicular
oval
ovate
palmate
pedate
peltate
pinnate
pinnatifid
plicate
reniform
rhomboidal
runcinate
sagittate
serrate
spatulate
subulate
ternate
trifoliate
tripartite
truncate

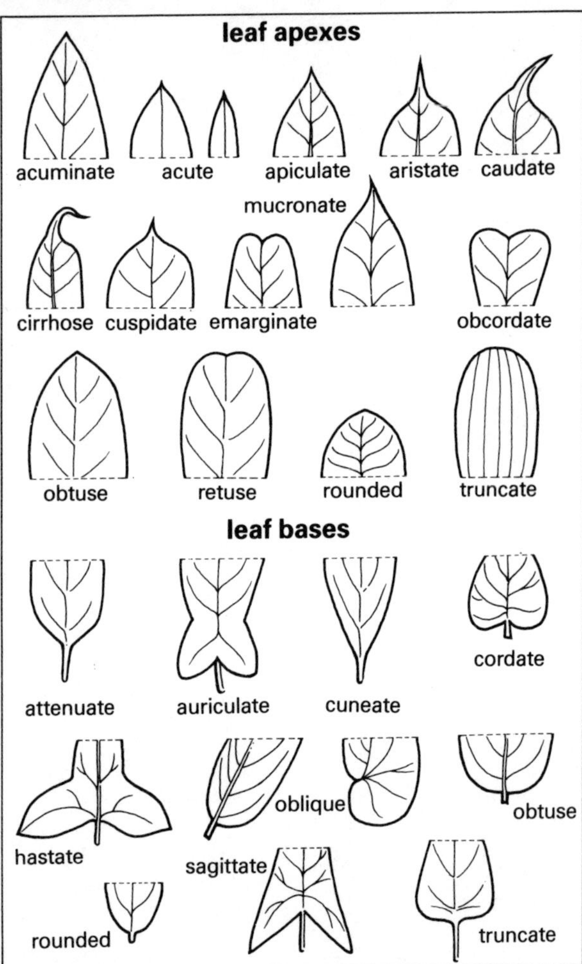
leaf apexes
acuminate
acute
apiculate
aristate
caudate
mucronate
cirrhose
cuspidate
emarginate
obcordate
obtuse
retuse
rounded
truncate
leaf bases
attenuate
auriculate
cuneate
cordate
oblique
obtuse
hastate
sagittate
rounded
truncate

organized colonies, and damage garden flowers (eg roses) by cutting pieces from the leaves for use in building the nests in which they lay their eggs. They usually cause only superficial damage.

leaf cutting n

a CUTTING made from a leaf or part of a leaf but without a growth bud attached. The leaf stalk is placed flat in a well-drained pan filled with a compost of peat, loam and sand. Roots develop from the leaf axil. Many greenhouse plants, eg *Begonia rex, Saintpaulia* and *Streptocarpus,* can be propagated by this method. Compare LEAF-BUD CUTTING.

leafhopper n

any of numerous small often brightly coloured insects that suck the juices of plants, often causing damage to crops and giving leaves a pale, mottled appearance. This can be controlled with MALATHION.

leaflet n

1 any of the parts into which a COMPOUND leaf is divided. **2** a small or young leaf.

leaf miner n

any of various small insects (eg moths and flies) that in the LARVA stage burrow into and eat the internal tissues of leaves, eg of chrysanthemums which are particularly vulnerable to this pest. Affected plants can be sprayed with HCH or the larva can be removed if it is visible under the skin of the leaf.

leaf mould n

1 a MOULD or MILDEW of leaves. **2** a compost or

soil layer composed chiefly of decayed leaves. This is rich in HUMUS and is extremely valuable as an addition to garden soil, contributing bulk and nutrients. It can be used as a TOP DRESSING or MULCH.

leaf roll n

a VIRUS DISEASE characterized by an upward and inward rolling of leaf edges, which results in stunted growth and a reduced yield. This is transmitted by the APHID.

leaf roller n

any of various moths and butterflies whose caterpillars make shelter by rolling up plant leaves.

leaf rust n

a plant disease caused by fungi and characterized by reddish-brown raised spots, chiefly on leaves. Infected leaves should be removed and burnt. Serious attacks should be sprayed with BENOMYL.

leaf scorch n

broadly, any condition that causes browning of the leaves of a plant. This is usually caused by faulty feeding, especially of fruit trees. Lack of POTASH is the usual deficiency, though the condition can also be caused (especially under glass) by dryness, sunlight and high temperatures, fumes from heating equipment, or use of an unsuitable spray or FUNGICIDE.

leaf spot n

any of various plant diseases caused by fungi and characterized by the appearance on the leaves of dark often circular spots.

leafstalk n

the stalk attaching a leaf to the stem of a plant.

leaf stripe n

any of various plant diseases characterized by striped discoloration of leaves.

leafsweeper n

a mechanical wheeled device designed to pick up fallen leaves, grass cuttings and general debris from a lawn. It is also useful for clearing paths and driveways.

lean-to n, pl **lean-tos**

a small building with a roof that rests on the side of a larger building or wall. See also GREENHOUSE.

leatherjacket n

the LARVA of the crane fly (daddy longlegs), which lives in the soil and causes serious damage to plants by feeding on their roots. It is very difficult to control but CONTACT insecticides may help.

leg n

the short stem on a shrub below the lowest branches.

leggy adj

(of a plant) spindly and having a bare lower stem.

legume n

1 strictly, the edible pod or seed of a LEGUMINOUS plant (eg a pea or bean) used as a vegetable. **2** any of a large family *(Leguminosae)* of plants, shrubs, and trees, including important food and storage plants (eg peas, beans and clovers) that bear fruits that are legumes.

leguminous adj

(consisting) of, resembling, or being a plant belonging to the family *Leguminosae.*

lenticel n

a pore in the stem of a woody plant through which gases are exchanged between the atmosphere and the stem tissues.

lepidate adj

(of a leaf) covered with tiny rough scales.

level vt

to make (an area of land) exactly flat or evenly sloped by removing soil from areas where there is too much and/or putting it into areas where there is too little. T-shaped wooden BONING RODS are pushed into the ground at regular intervals from the highest to the lowest points. By placing a spirit level on a board between the rods, discrepancies will be revealed and soil may be added or removed as necessary. Care must be taken not to remove all the TOPSOIL from any one area, thus bringing the SUBSOIL to the surface. If the land is very uneven, it is wise to remove the topsoil before commencing work, levelling the subsoil and replacing the topsoil afterwards. Levelling can be very strenuous work.

lichen n

any of numerous complex plants (group *Lichenes)* made up of ALGAE and FUNGUS growing in mutually beneficial association on a solid surface (eg a rock or tree trunk). Lichen can be controlled by spraying with a TAR-OILWASH.

lift vt

1 to dig up (a plant) for planting elsewhere. **2** to take up (bulbs and root crops) for storage.

light pruning n

1 the method of pruning a tree or shrub by cutting back old growth moderately in early spring before the new growing season begins. **2** the removal of dead flowers from a plant.

ligulate adj

(of a petal) shaped like a strap, eg the daisy petal.

ligule n

1 a scale-like or strap-shaped projection, eg the membranous outgrowth of a leaf, especially the sheath of a blade of grass. **2** the strap-shaped petals of a RAY FLORET forming part of a composite flowerhead, eg a daisy.

limb n

a large branch on a tree.

lime n

1 strictly, calcium oxide or quicklime. **2** broadly, the term is used by gardeners to refer to several substances containing CALCIUM. Lime is one of the main essentials for root fertility. It corrects acidity and 'sourness' in the soil and accelerates the decay of ORGANIC material. It checks pests such as SLUGS, LEATHERJACKETS or WIREWORMS, and makes clay soil coarser in texture, thus promoting drainage and aeration. In sandy soils, lime cements the soil particles, thus giving cohesion. Its calcium ingredient is an essential food for many plants; calcium deficiency

causes leaves to become stunted and to turn inwards.

The three main forms of lime used in the garden are:

1 Calcium oxide (burnt lime or quicklime). This is produced when chalk or limestone is burnt in a kiln. It is usually available in large lumps which, when placed on the soil, absorb moisture and fall to powder. It is not very pleasant to handle.

2 Calcium hydroxide (hydrated or slaked lime). This is burnt lime which has also been slaked down with added water. It is easy to handle and popular with gardeners, though it tends to scorch plant foliage.

3 Calcium carbonate (ground limestone and chalk). Limestone must be ground very fine to be effective in the garden. While chalk is usually soft enough not to need grinding, in some areas limestone contains magnesium carbonate and can therefore provide both calcium and magnesium.

Lime should be applied between October and February after digging. It should never be applied at the same time as other fertilizers or manure, as it reacts chemically with them or may make them less soluble and thus less effective. While regular applications of lime discourage certain diseases and pests, too much lime will encourage other diseases, eg potato scab, and may render certain nutrients, eg iron and manganese, unavailable. Ericaceous plants such as heathers, azaleas and rhododendrons, should not be given lime. See also ACID, ALKALINE, CALCICOLE, CALCIFUGE, CALCIUM.

[2]**lime** vt

to spread LIME (on the soil).

lime-hating plant n

see CALCIFUGE.

lindane n

see HCH.

linear adj

(of a bract, leaf or petal) having parallel sides and being at least twelve times longer than it is wide.

liquid fertilizer n

a highly concentrated form of COMPOUND FERTILIZER, particularly useful in the greenhouse and for houseplants. Liquid fertilizer is fast-acting but its effects are also short-lived.

liquid manure n

a liquid fertilizer derived from well-rotted FARMYARD MANURE. This has a high NITROGEN content and fairly rapid action. In a weak solution it may be used for feeding growing plants.

liquid sow vt

see FLUID SOW.

loam n

crumbly, reasonably fertile soil consisting of a mixture of clay, silt and sand.

lobe n

a curved or rounded projection or division on a leaf, BRACT, STIPULE or petal.

long-day adj

(of a plant) producing flowers only on exposure to long periods of daylight (such as in summer

periods), eg fuchsia. Compare DAY-NEUTRAL and SHORT-DAY.

lop vt

to prune (a tree) by removing or drastically cutting back its upper, large branches. There are various techniques of lopping. All should be carried out only when the tree is not growing actively, and should be undertaken with care to avoid damaging the tree's symmetry and shape.

Lorette system n

see SUMMER PRUNING.

lyrate adj

(of a leaf) shaped like a lyre, with the upper lobes much larger than the lower.

maculate adj
(of a flower or leaf) marked with spots or speckles.

magnesium n
a mineral that occurs abundantly in nature. It is essential to plants for the production of CHLOROPHYLL.

magnesium deficiency n
the lack of magnesium in the soil. A typical symptom in plants is the presence of white or pale green areas between the veins of green leaves. The remedy is to sprinkle SULPHATE OF MAGNESIUM into the soil and rake it in. Alternatively, spraying with a weak solution of sulphate of magnesium can have an instant effect. Magnesium deficiency rarely occurs where FARMYARD MANURE has been applied frequently.

maiden adj
(of a rose or fruit tree) being in the first year of growth after grafting or budding. A maiden tree usually consists of a single unbranched stem.

maintenance pruning n
to remove systematically from old fruit trees those branches that are not producing new growth. This removes diseased and infested wood and encourages new growth.

malathion n
a general-purpose insecticide used against sap-sucking garden pests such as GREENFLY.This is brown to yellow in colour and is available as a dust or spray. Though less toxic than many insecticides, it can injure certain plants eg ferns and various types of *Crassula* or *Petunia*.

male adj
(of a flower or plant) having stamens but no ovaries and not producing fruit or seed. The female counterparts may appear on the same plant (as in the hazel tree) or on separate plants (as with holly).

maneb n
a chemical fungicide used to control potato and tomato BLIGHT, BLACK SPOT and FUNGUS.

manganese n
a naturally occurring metallic element which is a TRACE ELEMENT essential for plant growth.

manganese deficiency n
the lack of manganese in the soil. A typical symptom in plants is the appearance of yellow speckles on the leaves. The deficiency can be corrected with applications of SEQUESTRENE. Manganese deficiency is most likely to occur in soil that has been well manured and contains excess LIME.

[1]**manure** n
any organic material that fertilizes land, especially animal excrement from stables and farmyards that is usually mixed with straw or

other forms of litter. There are several forms of manure, including FARMYARD MANURE and POULTRY MANURE, whose food value will depend on the animal concerned, the way the animal has been fed and stabled, and the length of time the manure has been stacked. Other organic matter, such as PEAT, LEAF MOULD and HOP MANURE, improves the soil texture but does not provide much in the way of nutrients. Dressings of manure are worked into the soil usually in the autumn and winter, or used as TOP DRESSING in spring and summer around fruit trees and bushes, roses and shrubs to conserve moisture. See also GREEN MANURE, LIQUID MANURE, SEWAGE SLUDGE, SHODDY.

[2]**manure** vt
to spread manure on (land).

marbled adj
(of a flower or leaf) having streaks or blotches of a different colour from the main colour, producing a surface effect considered similar to that of marble.

marcescent adj
(of a leaf) withering without falling off. This term is applied mainly to the leaves of deciduous trees, eg beech.

marcottage n
see AIR LAYERING.

margin n
the boundary or edge of a plant organ. The term is applied mainly to leaves.

marginal adj
1 *(of a plant)* requiring wet soil. Marginal plants

grow best at the edge of a pond. **2** characteristic of or occurring at a leaf margin.

marker plant n

a HERBACEOUS plant that can be seen in the winter above ground and serves as a reminder of nearby plants which are not seen during the dormant period.

marl n

a soil containing a fine-grained mixture of clay and silt and a high percentage of chalk. This is often used as a TOP DRESSING for soils that are deficient in lime, eg sandy or peaty soils.

May bug n

see COCKCHAFER.

meadow grass n

any of various grasses (eg of the genus *Poa*) that thrive in the presence of abundant moisture.

mealy bug n

any of numerous scale insects that have a white powdery covering and are destructive pests of greenhouse plants. Infestations may be controlled by spraying with MALATHION.

[1]medium n

a substance in which plants may be grown, eg a POTTING COMPOST or SEED COMPOST.

[2]medium adj

1 *(of soil)* being of good average quality. **2** *(of a flower)* being of a size between a large variety and a small variety.

menazon n

a SYSTEMIC insecticide used principally against APHIDS.This has a low level of toxicity to humans and domestic animals and is therefore quite safe to use. It should be applied at least 30 days before harvesting.

meristem n

a plant tissue that is the major area of growth, usually made up of small cells capable of dividing indefinitely and giving rise to similar cells or to cells that develop and become specialized to produce the definitive tissues and organs.

metaldehyde n

a chemical agent used to control slugs and snails. This comes in many variously formulated preparations and is harmful to pets and wildlife.

metamorphosis n

a marked change in the form or structure of an animal (eg a butterfly) occurring in the course of development.

mica n

any of various coloured or transparent silicon-containing minerals occurring as crystals that readily separate into very thin flexible leaves. See also VERMICULITE.

microclimate n

the essentially uniform local climate surrounding plants. This is partly determined by the design of the garden and layout of the beds.

micropropagation n

a technique of propagating plants from tip or leaf cuttings under laboratory conditions. A cutting is sterilized and placed in a nutrient gel in a sealed container until it has formed many new shoots; these are then divided into individual plantlets which can be either rooted or used to repeat the process. Thousands of plants, uniform and generally disease-free, can thus be produced from a single cutting.

microspecies n

a group of plants that resemble each other so closely that they are placed under one SPECIES heading, eg the various types of blackberry called *Rubus fructicosus.*

midrib n

the central vein of a leaf.

mildew n

any of various plant diseases characterized by a usually whitish growth on the surface of the plant and caused by parasitic fungi. Mildew is most likely to occur when the atmosphere is very moist and the soil dry. It can be controlled by use of a fungicide such as BENOMYL.

millepede, millipede n

any of numerous soil insects with long cylindrical bodies and a number of small legs. They can do extensive damage to a number of plants by burrowing into their roots, and they are difficult to control. Compare CENTIPEDE.

mimic vi

(of a plant) to resemble another object or plant. Some SUCCULENTS, for example, look like pebbles and some orchids like insects.

mineral n

any of various natural inorganic substances that are essential for plant growth. The three main minerals needed by plants are NITROGEN,

PHOSPHORUS and POTASSIUM. If they are lacking in the soil, they can be added in the form of fertilizers. Other elements, eg boron and iron, are needed in minute quantities and are known as TRACE ELEMENTS.

mineral deficiency n
the condition or result of having too little of one or more of the mineral elements necessary for normal growth. When these are insufficient plants will be noticeably affected.

mister n
an applicator used to provide a fine spray of liquid, especially to spray the foliage of indoor plants with water in order to increase humidity.

mist propagation n
a modern method of rooting HARDWOOD CUTTINGS in which a special light mist of water is sprayed over the cuttings in an open greenhouse. This method keeps the cuttings moist and prevents wilting without the usual need for maintaining a humid atmosphere, and it does not soak the root medium. The method is usually used in conjunction with soil-warming cables to provide the correct rooting temperature.

mite n
any of a large order of minute creatures related to spiders and ticks. Certain species are not true insects and are therefore unaffected by certain insecticides, which makes them difficult to control. These species can cause great damage to garden crops.

mixed adj
(of a border) containing a variety of plants including bulbs, annuals, perennials, shrubs, etc.

mole n
any of numerous small burrowing insect-eating mammals with minute eyes, concealed ears and soft fur. Moles do much good in the garden by devouring such soil pests as WIREWORMS or LEATHERJACKETS. Unfortunately, they also damage lawns and flowerbeds by burrowing under the surface and throwing up numerous mounds of loose soil (molehills). Moles can be dealt with by use of repellents, traps, poison or gas.

molybdenum n
a naturally occurring metallic element which is a TRACE ELEMENT essential for plant growth.

monocarpic adj
(of a plant) flowering only once before dying. ANNUALS and BIENNIALS are true monocarpic plants, but the term is also applied to those PERENNIALS, eg houseleeks and *Saxifraga longifolia,* that take several years to reach maturity and then die after flowering and seeding.

monocotyledon n
any of a group of flowering plants that have only one COTYLEDON, or seed-leaf, formed when the plant begins to grow from seed. Compare DICOTYLEDON.

monoecious adj
(of a plant) having separate male and female flowers on the same plant, eg the hazel.

monopodial adj
(of a plant stem) growing indefinitely from a single growing point and seldom branching. The term is usually applied to plants of the orchid family.

monotypic adj
(of a plant genus) having only one species, eg *Ginkgo* and *Rhoeo*. See CLASSIFICATION.

monstrous adj
(of a plant) having an extraordinary shape or size; deviating greatly from the natural form or character. Monstrous plants, eg those showing FASCIATION,are often prized by gardeners.

moraine n
an accumulation of earth and stones carried and finally deposited by a glacier. Certain ALPINES will only grow in these conditions of moisture and drainage, and moraine beds can be created by using small stone chippings with a water supply below. Compare SCREE.

mosaic n
any of several VIRUS DISEASES of plants characterized especially by diffuse yellow and green mottling or crippling of the foliage. Control is very difficult; plants should be burnt at the first sign of the disease.

moss n
any of a class of primitive, non-flowering plants having a very small leaf, often with tufted stem-bearing sex organs at its tip. Moss on lawns can be a serious weed; it can be controlled with various chemicals based on mercuric compounds.

moth n
any of numerous usually night-flying insects with antennae that are often feathery, larvae that are usually plant-eating caterpillars, and with duller colouring, shorter bodies, and proportionately smaller wings than butterflies.

mother adj
(of a tree or shrub) carefully raised to provide virus-free SCIONS for grafting purposes.

mould n
1 a superficial often woolly fungal growth that forms on damp or decaying plant tissue. **2** a fungus that produces mould.

mouse n
a small rodent with a pointed snout, rather small ears, an elongated body and a long, slender, almost hairless tail. Mice can be very destructive in the garden and greenhouse, feeding on bulbs and tubers, and eating the newly-sown seeds of crops such as peas and beans. Peas may be protected by rolling the seeds in paraffin and then in red-lead powder before sowing. Traps may help control mice in a greenhouse.

mow vt
to cut (lawn grass) with a LAWN MOWER.

Mowrah meal n
a mealy substance formerly used as a worm-killer on lawns. It is sprinkled on and watered in, causing the worms to come to the surface to die. It is seldom now used.

mucronate adj
(of a leaf) having a short, soft point at the apex.

[1]mulch n
a protective covering, such as COMPOST, MANURE, PEAT or other material spread on the ground around a plant to control weeds, enrich the soil and preserve moisture. See also BASE DRESSING, TOP DRESSING.

[2]mulch vt
to spread a mulch on (land).

muriate of potash n
a concentrated form of POTASH; an inorganic fertilizer which can be harmful to certain plants.

mushroom fly n
any of several species of small black flies, the larvae of which cause decay by eating into the stems of mushrooms.

mushroom mite n
any of several species of grey and white mites which tunnel into mushroom caps and stalks. They are usually introduced through the manure or growing medium.

mushroom mould n
any of certain fungi, both brown and white, which rob a mushroom crop of nutrients. Only one type of white mould will destroy the crop completely.

mutant n
an individual plant or STRAIN of plant differing from others of its type and resulting from a relatively permanent change in an organism's hereditary material. Also known as chimaera.

mutation n
the variation of a plant, usually caused by

chance, that produces a MUTANT. Also known as sport.

mycelium n

see SPAWN.

naturalize vt

to cause a plant to become established as if native.

neck rot n

see COLLAR ROT.

nectar n

a sweet liquid secreted by the flowers of many plants to attract pollinating insects. It is the chief raw material of honey.

net n

meshed material, usually of twine, cotton, polythene or nylon, used for protecting plants from birds, training climbing plants, shading greenhouses, forming windbreaks, etc.

neutral adj

(*of soil*) being neither ACID nor ALKALINE.

nicotine n

a poisonous substance derived from tobacco and often used as an insecticide, especially against APHIDS.

nitrate of potash n

an inorganic fertilizer containing both NITROGEN and POTASH in readily available form. It is useful for pot plants, but rather expensive for general garden use. It is better known as saltpetre.

nitrate of soda n
an inorganic fertilizer useful for the rapid release of NITROGEN and generally used as a TOP DRESSING.

nitro-chalk n
an inorganic fertilizer containing NITROGEN and LIME in readily useable form. It is clean and easy to handle and particularly useful on acid soils. It can also be used as an ACCELERATOR.

nitroform n
an inorganic nitrogen fertilizer that is released slowly. It is often an ingredient of rose and lawn fertilizers.

nitrogen n
a gaseous chemical element that constitutes about 78 per cent by volume of the atmosphere and is found in combined forms as a constituent of all living things. It is one of the three chief plant foods (along with PHOSPHORUS and POTASSIUM). and is generally responsible for the growth of leaves and stems.

nitrogen deficiency n
a shortage of the vital chemical element nitrogen that can cause stunted growth and paling foliage. Nitrogen deficiency occurs mainly in light soils.

nodal cutting n
a stem cut or pulled from the main shoot immediately below a node for the purpose of PROPAGATION.

node n
a point or joint on a stem at which one or more leaves are attached.

nursery bed n
a garden bed for raising young plants until they are mature enough to be transplanted to their permanent positions. It must be well drained, warm and kept moist.

nymph n
any of various immature insects, especially the LARVA of a dragonfly or other insect with incomplete metamorphosis.

obcordate adj
(of a leaf apex) comprising a pair of rounded lobes.

oblanceolate adj
(of a leaf) having a narrow base and broadening towards the tip.

oblique adj
(of a leaf base) having equal or slanting sides.

oblique side graft n
a type of graft used in FRAMEWORKING in which the SCION is cut as a pointed wedge and inserted into an oblique cut in a main branch at the angle in which it is intended to grow.

oblong adj
(of a bract, leaf or stipule) having parallel sides and a shape usually three times longer than wide.

oblong-orbiculate adj
(of a leaf) appearing almost round and nearly as long as it is wide.

oblong-ovate adj
(of a leaf) applying to an OBLONG leaf with sides curving in at either end.

obovate adj
(of a leaf) egg-shaped with the narrower end nearest the stalk.

obtuse adj
(of a petal or leaf) rounded or blunt at the apex.

oedema n
any abnormal amount of liquid in a plant tissue, the result of improper water balance. The condition generally occurs after overwatering.

offset n
1 a short shoot that grows out to the side from the base of a plant and produces new shoots and roots. **2** a small BULB arising from the base of another bulb. A result of natural VEGETATIVE PROPAGATION, it is easily removed from the parent bulb to become an individual plant.

oiler n
a special device which cleans garden tools by means of a felt pad supplied with oil from the plastic handle. It prevents corrosion of metal after use.

onion hoe n
a form of DRAW HOE with a short handle which is useful for weeding in restricted areas.

opposite adj
(of plant parts) having the points of attachment exactly across from (or opposite) each other. Compare ALTERNATE.

orbicular adj
(of a leaf or petal) flat and spherical; disc-shaped.

orchard n
an area of ground in which fruit trees (or occasionally nut trees) are planted.

orchid n
any of a large family of perennial herbaceous

plants that grow either in soil or as EPIPHYTES, and that usually have showy three-petalled flowers with an enlarged liplike middle petal.

organic adj
1 *(of a chemical compound)* being or composed of plant or animal matter and containing carbon compounds. **2** *(of gardening)* relating to, produced with, or based on the use of fertilizers of plant or animal origin without employment of synthetically formulated fertilizers or pesticides.

organic fertilizer n
any FERTILIZER that is made from material containing carbon compounds.

organic manure n
MANURE made from materials containing carbon compounds.

organic matter n
a substance consisting of decayed living organisms, eg COMPOST, MANURE.

ornamental adj
(of a plant) grown for beauty or pleasure rather than for use as timber or food.

oval adj
(of a leaf or petal) usually being rounded at the ends and one and a half times as long as it is broad.

ovary n
the enlarged, rounded, usually basal female part of a flower that bears OVULES and consists of one or more CARPELS.

ovate adj
(of a leaf or petal) having an egg-shaped outline,

widest at the base.

ovate-acuminate adj

(of a leaf or petal) basically OVATE in shape and ending in a long thin point.

ovate-cordate adj

(of a leaf or petal) having a basically OVATE shape with a heart-shaped base.

ovicide n

something that kills eggs, especially an insecticide effective against the egg stage.

ovoid adj

(of a fruit or bulb) egg-shaped.

ovule n

the small body within an OVARY which becomes the seed of a plant after fertilization. There are usually a number of ovules within the ovary.

oxygen n

a colourless, tasteless, odourless gas in the atmosphere, of which it forms about 21 per cent by volume, that is also found combined in water and in many organic compounds. It is essential for the life of plants and animals.

oxygenator n

a submerged AQUATIC plant that releases oxygen in ponds or pools to the benefit of other plants and livestock.

palmate adj
(of a leaf) having LOBES radiating from a common point, resembling a hand with the fingers spread.

pan n
1 a shallow pot used for raising seedlings. **2** a layer of hard soil forming as a result of frequent shallow cultivation at the same depth. **3** the layer of compacted clay or silt below the depth to which roots penetrate. Also called hardpan.

panicle n
a loosely branched flower cluster with numerous individually stalked flowers, eg lilac and buddleia.

paraquat n
an inorganic weedkiller which kills all forms of growth by destroying the green CHLOROPHYLL in plants. Repeated applications may be necessary to destroy deep-rooted perennial weeds. It is extremely poisonous, but has the advantage that it safely decomposes after a short while rather than persisting in the environment.

parterre n
a type of bedding scheme adapted to ornamental planting in gardens. It is best viewed from above as it is a geometric arrangement of beds separated

by a pattern of walks or grassy areas.

parthenogenesis n

reproduction by development of an unfertilized GAMETE, eg in the greenhouse banana, which is reproduced by SUCKERS.

patio n

a paved area adjoining a house, usually one that is sheltered and adapted to sitting outdoors. The bareness of a patio may be relieved by plants in containers.

PCNB n

a soil fungicide obtainable in dust or wettable powder forms. When worked into the soil it reduces bulb diseases and root rot. Cucumber, marrow and tomato seed should not be planted in soil treated with PCNB. Its scientific name is quintozene.

peat n

partially carbonized vegetable tissue formed by partial decomposition in water of various plants, such as mosses and sedge. It is found in large bogs and used as a fertilizer, being an excellent conditioner for poor soil although it does not provide many nutrients. CALCIFUGES thrive in peaty soil.

peat pot n

a small container formed from compressed peat, which can be filled with compost for growing seedlings. The entire pot can then be planted directly into the soil, avoiding the need for transplanting.

pedate adj
(of a leaf) shaped like a bird's foot, with deeply cut lobes.

pedicel n
a plant stalk that supports a fruiting or spore-bearing organ.

peduncle n
a plant stalk bearing a flower, flower cluster or fruit.

pelleted seed n
seed covered with a hard inert soluble coating, mainly consisting of clay, in order to make it easier to handle and sow at exact intervals.

peltate adj
(of a leaf) having the stem or support attached at the lower surface instead of at the base or margin, eg in the nasturtium leaf.

pendulous adj
(of a plant part) hanging downwards, or suspended so as to swing freely.

[1]**perennial** n
a plant that lives for several years. Plants of this type usually form the background of gardens in temperate climates.

[2]**perennial** adj
(of a plant) living for several years, usually with new HERBACEOUS growth each year, eg *Sedum spectabile.*

perfoliate adj
(of a leaf) having opposite leaves fusing together near the stem, so that in effect the stem passes through the leaf. Leaves of this type are often

found in honeysuckles and certain eucalyptus species.

pergola n
a garden structure originally designed as a narrow shaded passageway from one building to another or from one part of the garden to another, usually any structure with an open vine-clad roof, similar to an ARBOUR.

perlite n
a volcanic rock that expands on heating to form a lightweight sterile white granular material which can be used as an ingredient in composts or as a soil conditioner to improve drainage. It contains no nutrients. Compare ARCILLITE and VERMICULITE.

perianth n
the term used for the combination of petals and sepals when the two are indistinguishable from each other.

perpetual adj
(of a plant) blooming several times during the year, eg certain varieties of *Dianthus*.

pesticide n
any chemical, eg fungicide or insecticide, used to destroy insects or other garden pests (eg bacteria or rodents) attacking crops.

petal n
any of the modified, often brightly coloured leaves forming the COROLLA of a flower. Petals surround PISTILS and STAMENS and attract pollinating insects.

petal-fall adj
(of a bud stage) referring to the time after flowering and before the formation of fruit when nearly all of the petals have fallen.

petaloid adj
(of a plant part) resembling a petal in texture or colour, as in some modified SEPALS and STAMENS.

petiolate adj
(of a leaf) being attached to the stem by a LEAF-STALK.

petiole n
the usually slender stalk by which a leaf is attached to a stem; a leafstalk.

petroleum oil insecticide n
any of numerous PESTICIDES (including OVICIDES) made from petroleum oils. These are especially valuable for destroying moth eggs and RED SPIDER MITE in winter and suffocating SCALE INSECTS in summer.

pH n
the scale used as a means of measuring the acid-alkaline balance of the soil. The abbreviation stands for hydrogen ion concentration.

phosphate n
any of various salts of phosphoric acid which supply PHOSPHORUS, one of the three chief plant foods. Phosphates are quickly used up from the soil and BONE MEAL is a readily available source by which the supply can be replenished.

phosphorus n
a naturally occurring non-metallic element which

is, with NITROGEN and POTASSIUM, one of the three chief plant foods. It is made available to plants in the form of PHOSPHATE and is essential for root development.

photoperiodism n

the response of plants to the length of the day (strictly, length of night/darkness) specifically as it affects blooming.

photosynthesis n

the synthesis of organic chemical compounds from carbon dioxide and water using radiant energy, especially light, resulting in the formation of carbohydrates in the CHLOROPHYLL-containing tissues of plants exposed to light. This is the most important function of leaves, enabling them to make use of sunlight to form starch and sugar.

phylloclade n

a short stem fulfilling the function of a leaf. Compare CLADODE and PHYLLODE.

phyllode n

a flat, expanded leafstalk that resembles the blade of a leaf and fulfils the same functions. Compare CLADODE and PHYLLOCLADE.

picotee n

a flower, eg some carnations or tulips, having one basic colour and a margin of another colour.

pie n

see CLAMP.

[1]**pillar** n

a tree, usually apple, trained for a small, limited space. A pillar tree has an upright trunk with a succession of young fruit-bearing LATERAL shoots.

[2]pillar adj
(of a rose plant) being trained up the vetrical support of a PERGOLA or similar structure.

pilose adj
(of a plant organ) having long sparse hairs.

pinch back vt
to prune (young shoots of trees and shrubs) by plucking out the soft tips between forefinger and thumb. This form of pruning regulates growth and encourages the development of buds.

pinch out vt
to remove (the tips of unwanted shoots) in order to encourage new growth in the form of side shoots and to control flowering. Also called stop.

pink-bud adj
(of a bud stage) referring to the stage when flower buds are not yet open but display a trace of pink or white colour.

pinna n, pl **pinnae**
a leaflet or other primary division of a PINNATE leaf or frond.

pinnate adj
(of a leaf) resembling a bird's feather, especially in having similar parts arranged on opposite sides of an axis like the barbs on the shaft of a feather.

pinnatifid adj
(of a leaf) having a PINNATE arrangement in which the leaf is deeply cut into LOBES rather than formed of separate leaflets.

pinnule n
any of the secondary branches or divisions of a PINNATE leaf.

piping n
a young STEM CUTTING of a carnation or pink. The stem of a non-flowering shoot is pulled off just above a NODE. It needs no trimming and is inserted in sandy compost to root after being dipped in ROOTING POWDER.

piriform adj
(of a plant part) pear-shaped.

pistil n
the female reproductive organs of a flower, composed of one or more fused CARPELS and containing the OVARY, STIGMA and, sometimes, STYLE.

pistillate adj
(of a flower) having only female organs, ie PISTILS but no STAMENS.

pit n
a winter storage area for plants growing in containers that need protection from winter frost but do not require heat. A pit is usually dug about 6 ft (2 m) below ground and has brick walls, a dirt floor and a glass covering.

[1]**plant** n
1 any of a large number of living organisms typified by a lack of locomotive power or obvious nervous or sensory organs. **2** a tree, shrub, vine, flower, etc that can be placed in soil or other suitable medium for the purpose of natural growth.

[2]**plant** vt
to put (a plant) in the ground or soil for the process of growth.
planter n
a container, especially a decorative one, in which ornamental plants are grown.
planting tool n
any of various tools used for planting. A SPADE is necessary for trees, shrubs and large HERBACEOUS plants. A TROWEL may be used for smaller plants, for which a large DIBBER is also available, especially useful for vegetables. See also BULB PLANTER.
pleach vt
to interweave (branches) in order to form or renew a hedge.
plicata adj
(of a flower) being basically white or yellow with a marginal feathered pattern of another colour. This term is used specifically of the bearded iris.
plicate adj
(of a leaf) folded lengthways like a fan; ie pleated or ridged.
plumose adj
(of a plant organ) having a main shaft bearing small filaments. Also called feathery.
plumule n
the primary bud of a plant embryo that consists of leaves and a main stem and that develops into a shoot.
plunge vt
to set (a plant container) up to the rim in the soil

or in a bed of ashes, sand or peat. This prevents nursery plants from drying out rapidly and protects roots. It also makes it possible to LIFT them without the shock of TRANSPLANTING.

plunge bed n
a special bed of ashes, sand or peat in which plant containers may be placed for protection. The bed may be edged by boards standing above ground or can be made in a FRAME when overhead protection is needed.

[1]**pod** n
a long seed vessel or fruit, especially of the pea, bean or other LEGUMINOUS plant.

[2]**pod** vi
to produce pods.

[3]**pod** vt
to remove (seed vessels, eg peas) from a pod.

[1]**pollard** vt
to cut (all branches of a tree) back to the trunk. This is a brutal sort of pruning which produces a dense mass of foliage and extensive shoots.

[2]**pollard** n
a tree cut back to the main stem or trunk.

pollen n
the minute granular spores discharged from the ANTHER of the flower of a flowering plant, serve to fertilize the OVULES.

pollen sac n
any of the pouches of the ANTHER of a SEED PLANT in which pollen is formed.

pollination n
the first step in fertilization, in which pollen is

carried from an ANTHER to a STIGMA. This is usually accomplished by insects but can also be done artificially. See CROSS-POLLINATION and SELF-POLLINATION.

pollinator n

the agent of pollination, eg a bee or other insect or the wind.

pollinium n, pl **pollinia**

a coherent mass of pollen grains, often with a stalk bearing an adhesive disc that clings to an insect.

pompon n

a chrysanthemum or dahlia having small rounded flower heads with tightly packed petals.

[1]**pot** n

any of various rounded, square or oblong vessels used as plant containers. They can be made of a variety of materials, including clay, plastic, stone or peat.

[2]**pot** vt

to place (a plant) in a pot with soil for the purpose of growth.

potash n

any of various substances that contain POTASSIUM and which may be used to supply or increase potassium content in soil, eg as an ingredient of fertilizers.

potassium n

a naturally occurring metallic element which is, with NITROGEN and PHOSPHORUS, one of the three major plant foods necessary in the soil. It is contained in nearly all fertilizers, but especially those that stimulate flowering and fruiting.

pot-bound adj

(of a potted plant) having little or no space for further growth, as the roots have become densely matted in a pot too small for them.

potash/potassium deficiency n

a shortage of the mineral potassium in the soil, which can cause scorching of leaf edges, lack of fruit development and eventually death of plant parts. This occurs most often on peaty, chalky or sandy soils.

pot-grown adj

(of a plant) having been grown in a container.

pot-layering n

see AIR LAYERING.

pot on vt

to move (a plant) from one pot to another, usually from a smaller to a larger, to accommodate increased root development.

pot plant n

any plant placed in a container of soil for growth and protection.

potting n

the operation of planting (plants) in containers, sometimes also called potting-up or potting-off.

potting compost n

sterilized materials, usually including soil, peat, sand and other ingredients, for potting plants. Soilless compost, composed mainly of peat, is also available.

potting-off n

see POTTING.

potting shed n
a building in which POTTING is carried out. It usually includes a wooden bench and space for mixing potting composts and fertilizers.

potting-up n
see POTTING.

poultry manure n
poultry dung used to enrich soil with fertilizer materials. If dried, it has larger proportions of PHOSPHATES, NITROGEN and POTASH than if fresh. Pigeon manure is similar but richer.

powdery mildew n
a disease caused by a specific group of fungi, usually spread by wind-borne SPORES. It produces white powdery growth, usually on the upper surface of a leaf. In early stages the fungus may be rubbed off. It can be controlled by spraying with BENOMYL or another suitable fungicide. This disease may result in stunted growth, but rarely kills. Compare DOWNY MILDEW.

prickle n
see SPINE.

prick off vt
see PRICK OUT.

prick out vt
to transplant (seedlings) from the seed pan or pot in which they have been raised to other pots or receptacles that are larger and roomier. This is best done when their second pair of leaves – ie their first pair of true leaves – have appeared. Also called prick off.

procumbent adj
(of a plant) having prostrate stems that trail along the ground without rooting. Compare DECUMBENT.

propagate vt
to increase (plants) or create (new plants) from existing ones.

propagation n
1 the increase of plants. Natural means include SEMINAL PROPAGATION by seeds and spores and VEGETATIVE PROPAGATION,eg production of runners and offsets. **2** the creation of new plants from existing plants by any means. See BUD, CUTTING, DIVISION, GRAFT, LAYER.

propagation point n
the exact location at which new plants are obtained from the existing plant through one of the means of propagation.

propagator n
a device, usually a frame or case covered with glass or plastic, which retains air humidity and is thus useful for assisting propagation.

proximal adj
(of a plant part) next or nearest the point of attachment or origin. The term is often used in budding or grafting.

protoplasm n
the living material of a plant cell and its nucleus, consisting of a complex of organic and inorganic substances (eg proteins and salts in solution).

prune vt
to cut or trim (existing growth) on (usually

woody) plants for the benefit of that left on the shrub, tree or vine. This is done to promote flower and fruit production, to improve shape, or to remove dead or damaged wood. See also LOP, PINCH BACK.

pruners n
a cutting tool used to prune woody plants. Usually means the same as SECATEURS, although pruners can also be larger shears requiring the use of both hands.

pruning n
any method or process used to prune a plant. See also LIGHT PRUNING, MAINTENANCE PRUNING, ROOT PRUNING, SUMMER PRUNING, SPUR PRUNING, WINTER PRUNING.

pseudobulb n
a false bulb, usually occurring in orchids, appearing as a swollen, stem-like base. A pseudobulb can store food and water for the plant to use in the dry season.

puberulent adj
see PUBESCENT.

pubescent adj
(of a plant organ) covered with fine, short, soft hairs.

puddle-in vt
to coat (the roots of a plant) with thin wet soil before planting or transplanting. Although troublesome, this is especially beneficial in dry conditions.

pupa n, pl **pupae**
the intermediate, usually inactive, form of an

insect that undergoes metamorphosis; this occurs between the larval and adult stages. In moths, beetles and butterflies, the pupa is sometimes referred to as a CHRYSALIS.

pyramid n

a trained tree or shrub with a pyramidal outline. Apple and pear trees are often pruned in this shape. A tree pruned as a pyramid eventually becomes conical.

pyrethrum n

an insecticide derived from pyrethrum flowers. Available as a dust or a dry powder to be dissolved in water, it quickly destroys APHIDS and other garden pests and is non-toxic to humans and warm-blooded animals.

quicklime n
calcium oxide obtained by heating shells, limestone, etc. See LIME.

quintozene n
see PCNB.

raceme n
a simple stalk of flowers in which the flowers are borne on short side stalks of about equal length along an elongated main stem, eg lily-of-the-valley and wisteria flowerheads.

radical adj
(of a plant part) of or growing from the root or the base of a stem. The term is used especially of leaves.

radicle n
the first young root put forth from a seed; it is the lower part of the axis of a plant embryo or seeding, including the embryonic root.

raised bed n
a plant bed above ground level, usually constructed to promote good drainage. Raised beds can be walled with brick, stone or other materials or can simply consist of soil raised above the level of the ground. They are particularly useful for growing ALPINES and permit numerous plants to be grown in a small space.

[1]rake n
a tool with a number of prongs or teeth (usually ten or twelve) set in a crosspiece attached to a

long handle. The prongs enter the soil vertically for cultivation. See also LAWN RAKE.

[2]rake vt

to use (a rake) to level the ground, remove stones and debris and prepare beds for seeding.

rambler n

any of various climbing roses with long flexible stems and large clusters of rather small, often double, flowers.

ray floret n

one of the flat, marginal flowers in a flowerhead of a plant of the *Compositae* family, eg aster, daisy, sunflower, as distinguished from the tubular flowers in the central disc.

recurved adj

(of a plant organ) curving downwards and then usually in the opposite direction. The term is often applied to petals curving backwards from the face of the flower. Compare INCURVED, INTERMEDIATE, REFLEXED.

red spider mite n

an animal of the *Acarina* order, similar to a spider in that it has eight legs. It looks similar to a grain of rust, and lives on the underside of leaves. Like an APHID, it damages plants by sucking sap. It can often be destroyed with water as it thrives in a dry, hot atmosphere but is likely to develop immunity to insecticide.

reflexed adj

(of a plant organ) bending or curving sharply back on itself. The term is often applied to the petals of certain chrysanthemums and lilies. It classifies

organs that are more bent than those described as RECURVED. Compare INCURVED, INTERMEDIATE.

remontant adj

(of a plant) having a second flowering or fruiting season, as do many roses, some strawberries and other plants.

reniform adj

(of a plant organ) kidney-shaped. The term is used especially of leaves.

repot vt

to move (a plant) from one pot to another, usually to a larger pot or container. See also POT ON.

resting period n

the period when plants fail to develop growth, even if provided with heat and moisture and subjected to good treatment. In temperate climates this begins naturally in the autumn when trees and shrubs have completed their annual growth. See also DORMANT.

retard vt

to treat (plants) so as to hold back growth. This can be accomplished by placing flowering shrubs or bulbs in low temperatures. Chemicals are sometimes used to retard growth of fruit trees and hedges and cutting back can also cause retardation. Delaying growth is useful when blooms are desired in a certain season.

reticulate adj

(of a leaf or petal) having a branching network of veins on the surface, usually in a net-like pattern.

retuse adj
(of a leaf) having a rounded and notched end.

reversion n
1 the tendency of some hybrids to revert to their ancestral prototype. A grafted tree can produce SUCKERS which, if not taken off, will take over from the VARIETY grafted onto the tree. A MUTATION which is not genetically stable can also revert. **2** a VIRUS DISEASE of blackcurrants which causes smaller leaves and reduced crops. The disease is spread by aphids and there is no cure. Affected bushes should be destroyed.

rhizome n
an elongated, thickened and horizontal underground plant stem, distinguished from a true root in having buds and usually scale-like leaves.

rhomboidal adj
(of a leaf) having a diamond shape.

rib n
any vein on a leaf. Stems, such as those of cacti and various fruits, can also have ribs.

[1]**riddle** n
a meshed SIEVE.

[2]**riddle** vt
to sift or to separate (soil) with a riddle.

ridge vt
to cultivate heavy soil in winter to expose a greater area to the beneficial action of weather. Soil is removed from trenches and piled into steep parallel ridges. In spring the surface is levelled before planting.

rind graft n

see CROWN GRAFT.

ring vt

see BARK-RING.

ring culture n

a method of growing plants in bottomless containers. Only small amounts of soil are needed, so infection is uncommon. The containers are filled with potting compost and placed on a moist, easily drained bed of ashes, peat or sand. The bed is kept moist to accommodate deeper water-seeking roots.

rockery n

a natural or usually artificial bank of rocks and earth where rock plants are grown.

rock garden n

a garden laid out among rocks and adapted for the growth of particular kinds of plants (eg ALPINES).

rock plant n

a small plant (eg an ALPINE) that grows among rocks or is otherwise particularly suited to growing in a rock garden.

rogue n

any plant which is not true to its expected character, eg in colour. The term applies to varieties mixed by accident, and to naturally occurring MUTANTS.

roll vt

1 to level (a new lawn). **2** to firm and break down (lumpy soil) before planting. A roller may be used but treading is preferable in vegetable gardens.

roller n
a basic gardening tool, dating back to the 1500s. It consists of a cylinder mounted on a frame with a handle for pushing. It is very useful in the preparation and levelling of new lawns but can cause adverse conditions for grass roots in established lawns. A light roller can be useful in preparing seed beds.

[1]**root** n
1 the usually underground part of a flowering plant that provides anchorage and support for the plant, absorbs water and dissolved mineral salts from the soil, may function as a food storage organ, and differs from a stem especially in lacking buds and leaves. **2** an underground plant part (eg a true root or a BULB, TUBER or ROOTSTOCK), especially when fleshy and edible.

[2]**root** vi
to grow or establish roots.

[3]**root** vt
to cause (a cutting) to develop roots.

root aphid n
an APHID, generally grey, that sucks sap from the roots of a plant, often causing the plant to wilt and die. A suitable insecticide can be used or the plant can be removed from its pot and the roots washed in an insecticide solution or soapy water.

rootball n
see BALL.

root crop n
a crop (eg turnips or sugar beet) grown for its

enlarged fleshy edible roots.

root cutting n

a means of increasing plants, eg hollyhocks, which have fleshy or thick roots. A piece of root is cut into sections and planted vertically, lightly covered, in a deep box of soil. Some thin cuttings, eg phlox, can be placed horizontally under about $\frac{1}{2}$ in (1 cm) of soil.

rooting medium n

any substance, such as sand, in which a plant CUTTING can put down roots.

rooting powder n

a ready-made synthetic HORMONE, sold as a dust or powder, which is applied to a CUTTING, to assist in the rapid formation of roots. The end of the cutting is dipped in water and then in the rooting powder before being placed in potting compost. Also called hormone rooting powder.

root pruning n

the process of severing strong, thick roots in order to check overabundant growth and promote fruitfulness in fruit trees. Finer roots should not be pruned. The result of root pruning is a reduction in the flow of sap, which promotes fruit buds rather than leaf buds.

root rot n

root decay caused by the attack of various fungi. Black root rot attacks peas, pansies, violet, etc; violet root rot attacks carrots, asparagus, potatoes, etc. Honey fungus can cause root rot in a great variety of trees and shrubs. Affected plants should be removed and burned and the soil sterilized. Root decay can also be caused by poor soil conditions and waterlogging.

root run n

the area through which the roots of a plant extend.

root scorching n

damage to plant roots caused by the use of over-strong fertilizer in the soil near the roots.

rootstock n

1 an underground plant part formed from several stems. 2 a plant part used in GRAFTING consisting of (a piece of) root. Also known as stock.

rose n

a perforated fitting for the spout of a watering can, used to produce a finer and more widely distributed jet of water.

rose aphid n

a species of APHID which sucks the sap from roses. It checks and distorts growth and damages blooms. Regularly applied, some types of pesticide can control attacks.

rosette n

a cluster of petals or leaves arranged in a crowded circle or spiral, or in a rose-like pattern. Saxifrages and dandelions are examples of plants having leaf rosettes.

[1]**rot** vi

to undergo decomposition or decay, a process involved in several plant diseases.

[2]**rot** n

the appearance or condition of decay in a plant.

rotary cultivator n
an implement with blades or claws that revolve rapidly to till or break up the soil.

rotary mower n
see LAWN MOWER.

rotation n
a system by which different plants are grown on the same plot or soil in different years. This allows maximum use of soil resources and reduces the incidence of pests and diseases remaining in the soil and attacking the same plants. This system is more often used for agricultural crops and vegetable gardens than for ornamental plantings. For example, land which has been used to grow vegetables of the cabbage family in one year should preferably be given over to a different crop (eg beans or onions) in the following year.

rotenone n
a poison obtained from the roots of plants of the genus *Derris*, an active ingredient of the insecticide also called derris.

rounded adj
(of a leaf base or apex) having both sides equidistant from the stem.

runcinate adj
(of a leaf) having large downward-pointing teeth.

runner n
a weak, usually horizontal shoot that roots at the joints to form new plants. It grows above the soil and provides an easy method of propagation. Strawberries and violets are among the plants which produce runners.

russeting n
the scarring and roughening of the surface of fruit, and sometimes the cracking of the skin. It can be caused by frost, drought, mildew or inappropriate chemicals.

rust n
any of various plant diseases caused by many different fungi. The fungi are each specific to a certain group of plants. Such disease is recognized by rust-coloured spots on the leaf or stem. Some rust diseases require alternate hosts but others can thrive on only one. Not all of these diseases can be controlled with chemicals, but sometimes ZINEB is helpful.

saddle graft n
a type of graft in which ROOT-STOCK and SCION are of equal size. The scion contains one terminal bud. Both are cut to form an inverted V (or saddle) and the scion is fitted over the rootstock. The two are then bound together. Also **saddle graft** vt.

sagittate adj
(of a leaf) shaped like an arrowhead.

saltpetre n
see NITRATE OF POTASH.

sand n
loose granular particles smaller than gravel and coarser than silt that result from the disintegration of rocks; the best material to lighten heavy soil. Sand has no food value but improves the aeration of garden soils and composts and assists drainage in potting composts. Coarse sand–often known as sharp sand or silver sand–is an excellent rooting medium. The softer sand used by builders has little value in gardening.

sap n
the liquid in a plant; specifically the watery solution containing dissolved sugars, mineral salts

etc, that circulates through the conducting system of a plant.

saprophyte n

a plant that lives on a dead or decaying organism. Bacteria and fungi are the largest groups of saprophytes, but should not be confused with those that are parasites feeding on living organisms.

sawfly n

any of numerous fly-like insects whose grubs are garden pests. The female usually has a pair of saw-like serrated blades in her egg-laying organ. The LARVA resembles a plant-feeding caterpillar.

saxicolous adj

(of a plant) growing on or among rocks.

scab n

any of various fungus diseases characterized by crusted spots or cracks in plants. Apple and pear scab disfigures fruits and eventually attacks twigs and bark. A disease of this type can often be controlled by fungicide spraying. Potato scab is soil-borne and limeless soil can be beneficial, as can the liberal use of peat.

scalding n

a burning and browning of plant tissues resulting from heat, sometimes combined with intense light. This happens especially under glass and in greenhouses, where rapid changes of temperature, bright sunshine and certain fumes can cause direct damage to young leaves and fruit. It is recognized by white or brown spotting or by the withering of fruit. Tomatoes and grapes are particularly susceptible. Scalding can also occur in intense sunlight out of doors.

scale n

any small, often dry, modified leaf forming an appendage on a plant. Some cover growth buds or form bulbs. Also called scale-leaf.

scale insect n

any of various troublesome garden pests whose young suck plant juices. They firmly attach themselves to branches or bark and stay with the same host. Varieties include black scale, oyster-shell scale, oleandar scale, scurfy scale, mussel scale etc. They can often be removed with a knife, but insecticide is necessary if the attack is severe.

scale-leaf n

see SCALE.

scandent adj

(of a plant) climbing or ascending but not self-supporting.

scape n

a leafless flower stalk arising directly from the root of a plant.

scarify vt

1 to break up and the surface of (ground), eg by raking. **2** to cut or soften the coating of (a hard seed) in order to speed up penetration of water and thus hasten germination.

scion n

any bud or shoot removed from one plant to be grafted to another. It is usually selected for the quality of its fruit or flower and so usually forms the parts above ground in the resulting graft.

scissors n
a cutting tool with two blades pivoted so that their cutting edges slide across each other. Those used in the garden include blunt-ended scissors for flower gathering, special sharp pruning scissors and wire-cutting scissors.

scorching n
physiological damage, usually to leaves, caused by hot weather, strong sunlight, draughts, noxious fumes or insufficient water. Insufficient MAGNESIUM or POTASH and over-saturation with some fertilizers can also be the cause. Parts of the leaves turn brown and dry.

scrambling plant n
a fast-growing CLIMBER with long stems and often thorns that entangle with other plants growing close by, eg climbing roses, brambles and Russian vine.

scree n
a slope covered with loose stones or rocky debris. In gardens a small amount of loam is added. It is usually a feature of a rock garden and should not be confused with a MORAINE, which is provided with an underground water system.

screen n
a fence, hedge, trellis or wall that encloses a garden or part of one. This can be useful as a windbreak, for concealing an ugly view, for safety or as support for climbers and creepers.

seaweed n
sea vegetation which is useful as a MANURE. It is a good source of NITROGEN, PHOSPHATES

and POTASH. When dried it may be buried or dug into the soil in a quantity of about 3 lb to the square yard ($1\frac{1}{2}$ kg per square metre). If it is not first dried, a greater weight is needed in the same area. See also ALGINATE.

secateurs n

small shears used for pruning. There are two basic types: the anvil type, which has a single flat-edged blade cutting onto a metal or plastic anvil, and the parrot-beak or bypass type, which has two curved blades cutting with a scissors action.

[1]**seed** n

1 the sexual (as opposed to vegetative or asexual) means of a plant's propagation. **2** the fertilized ripened OVULE of a flowering plant that contains an embryo and is capable of GERMINATION to produce a new plant. **3** the grains or ripened ovules of plants used for sowing.

[2]**seed** vi

1 to sow seed. **2** *(of a plant)* to produce or shed seeds.

[3]**seed** vt

1 to plant seeds in. **2** to plant (seeds) in the ground for growth.

seed compost n

ready-mixed compost specially formulated for growing seedlings, containing the nutrients necessary for healthy growth.

seed leaf n

see COTYLEDON.

seedling n
1 a recently germinated young plant, usually with a single, soft, unbranched stem. **2** a plant grown from seed rather than from a CUTTING.

seed pan n
any shallow container in which seed can be planted for GERMINATION, usually available in plastic or wood. It need be no more than 2 in (5 cm) deep.

seed plant n
a plant (eg a flowering plant or conifer) that bears seeds.

seed sower n
a usually hand-held container with a spout through which seeds are shaken into a prepared DRILL.There are also wheel-mounted versions which can be pushed over a prepared seed bed; these are designed to open up and fill in the drill as the seed is sown.

selective weedkiller n
any weedkiller that kills certain unwanted plants while leaving other surrounding plants unharmed, eg DALAPON.

self-clinging adj
(of a climbing plant) having TENDRILS or aerial roots that enable it to cling to a wall, fence or other vertical surface without the use of stakes or a trellis.

self-coloured adj
(of a flower) having a single colour.

self-fertile adj
(of a plant) capable of fertilizing with its own

pollen, ie no pollinating partner is needed.

self-fertilization n
see SELF-POLLINATION.

self-pollination n
pollination of a plant with its own pollen.

self-sterile adj
(of a plant) requiring a pollinating partner for fertilization (in order to produce seeds and fruits).

semi-double adj
(of a flower) having more petals than the average or the wild species. Compare DOUBLE, SINGLE.

semi-evergreen adj
(of a tree or shrub) retaining most of its leaves during a mild winter, although tending to shed them in severe weather.

seminal adj
(of a plant part) consisting of, storing or conveying seed.

seminal propagation n
the increase of plants by sexual processes, eg through seeds and spores contained within the original plant.

sepal n
any of the modified leaves comprising the CALYX of a flower.

sequestrene n
a mixture of organic chemicals used to correct mineral deficiencies in the soil, especially iron deficiency. Also known as a chelated compound.

serpentine layering n
a method of layering in which long flexible stems or shoots, eg those of the clematis, are covered

with soil at intervals. In some cases oblique cuts are made in the stems near nodes where roots are to form.

serrate adj

(of a leaf) notched or having saw-like teeth on the edge.

sessile adj

(of a leaf or flower) attached directly by the base without a stalk.

[1]**set** n

1 a young plant or rooted CUTTING ready for transplanting. **2** a small BULB, CORM or piece of TUBER used for PROPAGATION. The term is used especially in relation to an onion or shallot.

[2]**set** adj

(of blossom) pollinated and on its way towards producing fruit or seed.

sewage sludge n

human excreta which has been processed in sewage works. It is sometimes used instead of MANURE but, unless dried, can be unpleasant to work with. It is rich in NITROGEN and PHOSPHORUS.

[1]**shade** n

partial darkness caused by the interception of rays of light.

[2]**shade** vt

to shelter or screen (plants) by intercepting radiated light or heat. Although light is needed by all green plants, some need less than others, and many need shade during some stage of development. Greenhouses are sometimes shaded with canvas, bamboo, paper or other materials. Plants may also be shaded with screens, walls and hedges.

shears n

a gardening tool which resembles large strong scissors with long blades. Some have refinements such as hollow-ground blades, easy blade adjustment, shock absorbers and a pruning notch at the base of the blades. There are also lighter models, one-handed models for trimming grass, and long-handled models with angled blades for edging.

sheathing adj

(of a leaf) having a base which forms a tubular shape around the stem.

shelter n

any means of protecting plants from extreme weather conditions. Greenhouses, glass, hessian, coverings of straw and netting are all means of shelter for plants.

shelter belt n

a planting of shrubs or trees as a windbreak or as a protection for other plants. It often resembles a tall, very thick hedge. It is used by gardeners in windswept (and especially seaside) areas, but more extensively by farmers around cropping areas.

shingle n

coarse water-worn pebbles, obtained from the sea, often used in greenhouses as a surface for STAGING.

shoddy n

a bulky organic MANURE often used to break up

heavy soil. It is obtained as waste from wool factories and, though slow to rot or decay, is a valuable source of NITROGEN.

shoot n

1 a sending out of new growth or the growth sent out. 2 a stem or branch with its leaves, buds etc; especially when not yet mature.

short-day adj

(of a plant) producing flowers only on exposure to short periods of daylight (strictly, long periods of night/darkness, such as in winter periods), eg chrysanthemum. Compare DAY NEUTRAL, LONG-DAY.

shot-hole disease n

a bacterial disease that causes circular holes in leaves, decay in bark and slimy soft rot (the latter usually in celery or cabbages). It also causes CANKER in cherries. If used carefully, COPPER FUNGICIDE sprays can control this disease.

shrub n

a low-growing usually several-stemmed woody plant.

shrubbery n

an area of ground in which a collection of shrubs is planted.

side graft n

a type of GRAFT used in FRAMEWORKING in which a SCION with unequal sides is inserted into a main branch at an angle of 20 degrees. Also **side graft** vt.

side shoot n

a LATERAL GROWTH, branching from the main stem.

[1]sieve n
a device with a meshed or perforated bottom that will allow the passage of liquids or fine solids while retaining coarser material. It is used to remove debris, rocks, twigs and clods in the preparation of soil.

[2]sieve vt
to sift (soil) with a sieve.

silt n
a loose material that results from the weathering of rocks and consists of particles that are coarser than those of clay but finer than those of sand.

simazine n
a TOTAL WEEDKILLER, especially suited to use on pathways or for application to clean ground to prevent weed seedlings. It may also be used selectively to control weeds in rosebeds and between berry rows. It is usually effective for a year and does not spread sideways through the soil.

[1]single adj
(of a flower) having the normal number of petals for the species. Compare DOUBLE and SEMI-DOUBLE.

[2]single vt
see THIN OUT.

single dig vt
to dig (soil) to the depth of one SPIT; the oldest and simplest method of turning the soil before planting. The main objects are to loosen the soil, allow it to breathe, and to cover up all weeds and spent manure. Compare DOUBLE DIG, TRENCH.

sinuate adj
(of a leaf) having a wavy edge with strong indentations.

slow-release adj
(of a fertilizer) releasing nutrients over a long period of time; dissolving slowly in the soil. Also called controlled-release.

slug n
any of numerous slimy elongated chiefly ground-living gastropod molluscs that are found in most damp parts of the world. They have no shells or only rudimentary ones. Slugs feed on roots and plants above ground, often destroying small plants and seedlings. Almost impossible to eliminate, they can be controlled. The best methods are SLUG PELLETS, LIME, common salt or physical destruction after dark.

slug pellets n
ready-made poison bait which acts against slugs, usually containing concentrated metaldehyde.

Smith period n
the time of high humidity after rainfall which, in combination with specific temperatures, can cause SCAB infection of apples.

smokes n pl
fungicides, insecticides or both packaged in such a way that when ignited they emit chemicals into a greenhouse. To prevent fumes escaping, the greenhouse should be made as air-tight as possible. Burning NICOTINE is a more old-fashioned form of the same process.

smuts n
any of various destructive fungus diseases, especially of cereal grasses, marked by the transformation of plant organs into dark masses of spores. Infected plants should be destroyed and COPPER FUNGICIDE can be tried as a means of prevention.

snag n
a stump or stub of a branch that is too small to bear leaves, usually left projecting from a trunk or limb by poor pruning or after breakage.

snail n
a gastropod mollusc with an external shell. It feeds on plants and shelters on walls, under rocks and in protected places. Control is similar to that used for the SLUG, and physical removal is most effective.

sodium chlorate n
a non-selective TOTAL WEEDKILLER which destroys plants and weeds of all types. It is most useful on paths and drives, keeping them clear for at least six months. It travels through the soil and remains effective for an extensive time, but can be a fire risk.

soft fruit n
edible fruit (eg strawberries, raspberries. gooseberries, currants) that is small, stoneless, and grows on low bushes. Also known as BUSH FRUIT. Compare TOP FRUIT.

soft rot n
any of a number of bacterial and fungal diseases which cause decay of plant tissues. Plants usually

become slimy or soft. Too much NITROGEN in MANURE encourages these diseases, as does excessive humidity, especially in plants grown under glass. Root crops and fruits in storage can also be attacked and should be discarded.

softwood cutting n

a method of plant PROPAGATION by removal of a young, soft, green stem with no woody tissue. Cuttings should be about 2 in (5 cm) long and should be kept moist and warm until roots have formed.

soil n

the land or earth, especially the upper layers, in which plants may grow. It is the source of all food which the plant does not get from the atmosphere and the only food supply which can be controlled or improved by the gardener, eg by the addition of fertilizers.

soil block n

a block of compressed soil used for PROPAGATION of plants. Some of the work involved in using pots is avoided through use of blocks, but very careful watering is necessary.

soil-borne adj

(of a plant disease) transmitted by or in the soil.

soil capacity n

the maximum amount of water soil can contain without becoming waterlogged. Well-drained soil is usually at capacity in March, barring a dry winter.

soilless compost n

a growing medium for seeds, cuttings and potted

plants which contains no soil but instead is based on other materials such as peat or sand.

soilless culture n
any method of growing plants without the use of soil. Nutrient solutions, including water, sand, gravel and peat, are used instead of soil. Plants are usually kept upright by wire frames. Soil-borne diseases and deficiencies can be avoided and maximum control of plant growth obtained.

soil moisture deficit n
the amount of water it is necessary to add to soil to bring it back to capacity. See SOIL CAPACITY.

soil testing n
any means of determining the nutritional value of the soil. The chemical balance, the texture and the PH (acidity) are of vital interest to the gardener. County horticultural advisers will conduct tests or home-testing kits can be purchased, though the latter are generally less accurate.

soil warming n
the application of warmth from below plants. Methods include electric heating cables or hot water pipes placed beneath the soil. The most commonly used and inexpensive method is to grow plants in a frame over a heap of fermenting MANURE. See also BOTTOM HEAT.

soot n
a fine black powder consisting chiefly of carbon separated from various fuels during combustion. It forms a smutty nuisance often detrimental to

growth of plants in city gardens. However, soot can be valuable as a fertilizer containing NITROGEN. If used as such it must be dried for at least four months to destroy its dangerous impurities.

sooty mould n

a dark mould caused by a fungus that develops on the excreta of pests such as SCALE INSECTS. It can hinder the natural growth of the plant. The pests should be eradicated and the mould removed with soapy water.

sour adj

(of soil) excessively acid, and usually poorly drained.

sow vt

to plant seed for growth, especially by scattering.

spade n

a digging implement that can be pushed into the ground with the foot. A spade usually consists of a piece of metal flat at the top and sometimes rounded at the bottom, at the end of a straight handle. Many different types of spade are available, with the metal of different shapes and at different angles to the handle.

spadix n

a spike of crowded flowers with a fleshy or succulent axis, usually enclosed in a SPATHE.

spathe n

a sheathing BRACT or pair of bracts enclosing the flowers of a plant, especially a SPADIX on the same axis. In palms it is usually woody; in AROIDS it is leafy.

spatulate adj
(of a leaf or petal) spatula-like in shape, with one end rounded and broad and the other narrow.

spawn n
1 the thread-like growths of a FUNGUS which may produce edible fruits, eg in the mushroom. Also called mycelium. 2 tiny root developments of fleshy-rooted plants which eventually form true roots.

species n
a group of individual plants with the same general characteristics. A category in the biological CLASSIFICATION of plants that ranks immediately below a GENUS and the members of which are capable of interbreeding.

specimen plant n
a plant in perfect condition, usually planted alone so that it may be shown off and observed.

sphagnum moss n
any species of a large genus of atypical mosses that grow only in wet, acid areas where their remains become compacted with other plant debris to form peat. It is useful for its capacity to combine water-retaining properties with good drainage. Also called bog moss.

spike n
an elongated plant INFLORESCENCE with the flowers stalkless on a single main axis.

spine n
a sharply pointed usually woody structure, usually a modified branch, leafstalk or flower stalk. A thorn or prickle is a form of spine.

spit n
the depth of soil dug with a fork or spade, usually about 12 in (30 cm).

splice graft n
a type of GRAFT used for tender wood and small shoots. SCION and ROOTSTOCK are both cut diagonally and simply tied together. A pin can be inserted vertically in the stock for firmness. Also called whip graft. Also **splice graft** vt.

spore n
a primitive usually single-celled hardy reproductive body produced by plants, bacteria and fungi and capable of development into a new individual either on its own or after fusion with another spore. Ferns are the only common garden plants to reproduce by means of spores.

sport n
see MUTATION.

[1]**spray** n
1 a group of flowers on one stem. **2** fine droplets of liquid, eg water or chemical solution, blown through the air. **3** a mechanical device capable of converting a liquid into a spray of droplets.

[2]**spray** vt
1 to apply (chemical spray) to plant foliage to destroy insects or fungi. **2** to apply (water as a spray) to prevent drooping or wilting.

spray damage n
plant injury caused by too-heavy dosages of sprayed chemicals which harm foliage or fruit. Soft foliage and extreme temperatures (low or high) promote such injury.

sprayer n
any applicator used to spray plants.

sprinkler n
a device attached to a hose, to produce a spray of liquid, especially water. The simplest types have no moving parts and consist of a plastic or metal nozzle, attached to an earth spike, which directs a curtain of spray. More complicated versions have revolving heads which distribute a fine spray over a larger area.

[1]**sprout** n
1 any young shoot, particularly on a germinating seed. **2** a growth on a TUBER, eg the eye of a potato.

[2]**sprout** vi
to produce a young shoot or other sprout.

spur n
1 a short branch bearing close, often twisted clusters of fruit buds. On more mature trees, these sometimes become large and heavy and need trimming. **2** a hollow projection from a plant's petals or sepals in which NECTAR is sometimes produced (eg in the columbine).

spur pruning n
the practice of cutting back LATERAL shoots to two or three growth buds. This is commonly used on apple trees to encourage the production of clusters of fruit or flower buds which form spur growths.

stage n
one section of the STAGING in a greenhouse.

staging n
the system of table-like shelves in a greenhouse for the arrangement of plants above soil level. The main stage is often waist high, and tiered staging is also often used. Staging is sometimes constructed of slats arranged with space between them. A solid surface of sand, gravel or peat can be applied when humidity is desirable.

[1]**stake** n
a piece of wood, bamboo cane or other rigid material used to support a plant. It is placed alongside the stem of a plant, which is then tied to it.

[2]**stake** vt
to place (a stake) alongside a plant for support.

stalk n
1 the main stem of a non-woody plant, often with its attached parts (eg leaves). **2** a stem carrying an individual leaf, flower or flowerhead.

stamen n
the organ of a flower that produces the male GAMETE in the form of POLLEN, and consists of an ANTHER and a FILAMENT.

staminode n
an infertile STAMEN. It often resembles a true stamen but produces no pollen. Some are petal-like, eg in certain peonies.

stand n
a group of plants, especially trees, growing in a continuous area.

standard n
1 the uppermost petal, or group of petals, of a

flower. It is easily recognized in the iris and in pea flowers. **2** a tree or shrub having a main bare stem and in which the growth is concentrated in a terminal crown of foliage and blooms. Compare HALF STANDARD.

[2]**standard** adj

(of a plant, tree or shrub) being in the form of a standard, eg a standard rose.

start vt

to bring (a plant) into new growth after a dormant period. This applies mainly to bulbs, CORMS or TUBERS which can be started by giving warmth and water after planting.

stellate adj

(of a leaf or flower) star-shaped.

stem n

1 the main trunk of a plant above ground, specifically a primary plant axis that develops buds and shoots. **2** a branch, PETIOLE or other plant part that supports leaves, fruit and shoots.

stem cutting n

a cutting taken from the tip of any stem or branch. It can be classified as a HALF-RIPE, HARDWOOD, or SOFTWOOD CUTTING. Also called a top cutting.

stem-rooting adj

(of a plant) producing roots above ground, eg some climbers, lilies, and plants with PROSTRATE stems.

stem rot n

any disease which attacks the stems of plants and causes their decay.

stepover n
a fruit tree trained as a low espalier with a single pair of arms so that it can be used as an edging plant.

sterilant n
any agent used for sterilizing.

sterile adj
1 *(of a plant)* unable to produce seed; often true of a MUTANT or HYBRID. **2** *(of a planting medium)* referring to POTTING COMPOST which is sterilized by heat or chemical means to destroy harmful organisms or to media used in SOILLESS CULTURE unlikely to contain disease.

sterilization n
the act of destroying unwanted fungi, bacteria and seeds in the soil. Ideal soil is only partially sterilized, as some bacteria are beneficial. Heat and chemicals are the most commonly used methods of sterilization.

stigma n
the portion of the female part of a flower which receives the POLLEN grains and on which they GERMINATE.

stipule n
a small appendage at the base of the leaf in many plants, eg roses.

stock n
1 see ROOTSTOCK. **2** a plant grown specifically to produce ROOTSTOCK.

stolon n
a runner or horizontal branch from the base of a

plant that produces new plants (as in the strawberry).

stone n

the hard-coated seed of any member of the *Prunus* family (cherry, peach, apricot etc). Adequate plant food and moisture are necessary for forming a stone, without which the fruit will not develop.

[1]**stool** n

1 the ROOTSTOCK of a plant that develops numerous shoots from the roots and is capable of simple DIVISION. **2** a shoot or other growth growing from a tree stump or plant crown.

[2]**stool** vt

to cut down (a plant) to its base in order to induce it to throw out new shoots from a stump or crown. Eucalyptus trees, for example, are often treated in this way every year so that they produce their attractive juvenile foliage.

stop vt

see PINCH OUT.

storage rot n

any disease which attacks roots or fruits that are stored. This can be caused by bruising or by failure to clean off soil. Decaying fruits should be removed to keep the rot from spreading.

stove n

a hothouse, especially one for the cultivation of exotic tropical plants. Also used, loosely, for a greenhouse.

strain n

a category of plants within a variety. Usually some characteristic makes a strain different enough to hold a designation but insufficiently distinct to be worth calssifying as a separate variety. A strain is always raised from seed.

strap-shaped adj
(of a leaf) long and parallel-sided, usually three times as long as wide.

stratification n
the process of speeding up the GERMINATION of fleshy or hard seeds through exposure to frost or low temperatures before sowing. Stratification softens the hard seed coats. The seeds are usually placed in the refrigerator or during winter may be put in pots of sand or peat and placed outdoors, when they should be covered with netting to protect them from birds. Compare VERNALIZATION.

streak n
a serious VIRUS DISEASE which produces black or brown streaks on the stems or leaves of a plant. Sweet peas and tomatoes are particularly susceptible and the fruit of the latter can be affected.

strike vt
to root (cuttings) successfully.

strobilus n
a small cone-like mass of scales and their fruits, eg a pine cone.

stub n
1 a short piece of broken or cut branch on a main stem. **2** the stump of a tree rooted in the ground is also sometimes referred to as a stub.

stub graft n
a type of graft used in FRAMEWORKING in which the SCION is grafted onto a stub or spur of a lateral branch as close to the main branch as possible. Also **stub graft** vt.

[1]**stunt** vt
to hinder or arrest the growth or development of (a plant); to DWARF.

[2]**stunt** n
1 a check in growth. **2** a plant disease in which dwarfing occurs.

style n
a prolongation of a plant OVARY bearing a STIGMA at the top.

sub-alpine n
a plant native to the lower slopes of the Alps, capable of growing on the high upland slopes below the tree line.

sub-shrub n
a PERENNIAL partly woody plant producing soft growth which may die down in the winter.

subsoil n
the layer of soil below the fertile TOPSOIL. Its character affects the quality of the topsoil. It is usually composed of clay, chalk or gravel.

sub-tropical adj
(of a plant) originating in the geographical regions bordering on the tropical zone. Frost will destroy such plants, but they can sometimes be grown out of doors in a temperate climate during warm times of the year.

subulate adj
(of a leaf) narrow and tapering to a fine point.

succulent n
any plant with fleshy, thick stems or leaves which can store water. It has adapted this mechanism to survive in arid, dry conditions, eg cactus or stonecrop.

sucker n
a shoot arising from below ground at the base of a plant, usually directly from the roots. This can be a distinct problem on grafted plants as such shoots will resemble the ROOT-STOCK rather than the SCION. Suckers should be removed by pulling them off at their point of origin on the roots.

sulphate of ammonia n
a quick-acting inorganic fertilizer which is an excellent source of NITROGEN. It is an ingredient of numerous compound fertilizers and may be used alone as a TOP DRESSING.

sulphate of copper n
an extremely strong fungicide which may be used in winter but which will cause severe leaf scorching if it contacts foliage. Mixed with LIME it produces the popular fungicide BORDEAUX MIXTURE.

sulphate of magnesium n
a prepared substance containing a percentage of MAGNESIUM, used to correct deficiencies of magnesium indicated by yellow foliage. It may be sprayed in solution or applied to the soil directly. Also called Epsom salts.

sulphate of potash n
a quick-acting inorganic fertilizer high in POTASH content. Used alone to improve fruitfulness or as a component of compound fertilizers, it can be sprayed onto foliage or applied as a TOP DRESSING.

sulphur n
1 a nonmetallic element which is a TRACE ELEMENT essential for plant growth. **2** a powerful fungicide particularly useful against MILDEW and also pests such as MITES. It can be applied in a dust form or as a spray. Sulphur candles for greenhouse fumigation are also available. Some fruits are sulphur-shy and their foliage can be damaged by its use.

summer chafer n
a beetle which is often seen flying just after dusk on a summer evening and which makes a buzzing noise. Both the larvae and the adult insects destroy the leaves and roots of plants.

summer pruning n
a system of pruning in the summer months, used particularly on fruit trees. It prevents excessive growth and induces the formation of fruit buds for the next season. LATERAL shoots are usually cut back to about five leaves. Also called the Lorette system.

superphosphate of lime n
an inorganic fertilizer which is rich in PHOSPHATES and is very useful as a BASE DRESSING before planting in spring or early summer. It is a common ingredient of compound

fertilizers. The term lime is misleading as this fertilizer will not affect soil acidity. Triple superphosphate is a highly concentrated form of the same.

[1]**support** n

any means of holding plants upright. Plants requiring support include young trees and shrubs, tall, brittle plants, climbers and scrambling plants. Vertical stakes for trees, shrubs and upright plants may be wood, bamboo, metal, plastic or anything strong enough for the purpose. Climbing or scrambling plants can be trained on a PERGOLA, wall or trellis, while plants such as peas and beans can often be supported by twiggy branches.

[2]**support** vt

to provide (plants) with a means of growing upright.

sward n

a piece of ground covered with short grass.

sweet adj

(of soil) alkaline or neutral; not acid.

swelling adj

(of a bud stage) referring to the time when the bud enlarges and the bud scales begin to separate.

symbiosis n, pl **symbioses**

the living together of two dissimilar organisms in intimate association to their mutual benefit. Many fungi, for example, live together with the roots of other plants, each contributing to the nutrition of the other.

symphilid n
a centipede-like creature with twelve pairs of legs and fourteen body segments. It destroys plant roots, often causing stunting in tomatoes, and leads to MILDEW in many plants. Treatment with insecticide is usually effective.

synonym n
in botanical terms, an alternative plant name, usually the result of reclassification or of a plant having been named by two people.

synthetic fungicide n
a man-made FUNGICIDE, one that does not exist naturally.

synthetic insecticide n
a man-made INSECTICIDE, one that does not exist naturally.

syringe n
a form of sprayer, a device for applying water, liquid fertilizer, fungicide or pesticide to plants. A plunger pulls liquid from a bucket or cylinder and pushes it out.

systemic adj
(of a fungicide, herbicide or insecticide) referring to a chemical compound which enters the plant sap when watered on the soil or sprayed on plants. In this way a systemic insecticide destroys sap-sucking insects, as well as those that feed on the surface. Many such compounds are poisonous to humans and animals so instructions should be followed carefully.

tap root n
any strong, usually fleshy root that descends vertically and often feeds deeply. The term is applied to the chief anchoring root of a plant, particularly of trees or root vegetables (carrots, parsnips etc) which have edible roots.

tar oil wash n
an inorganic preparation used as WINTER-WASH for the purpose of destroying the eggs of scale insects, hibernating caterpillars and APHIDS.It is usually used on fruit trees, but often on roses and other shrubs, and is also used for cleaning moss and lichen from tree bark. It causes great damage to foliage and is thus always applied when plants are dormant during winter.

taxonomy n
the study of the principles of scientific CLASSIFICATION of plants and animals, according to their presumed natural relationships. See CLASSIFICATION.

temperature n
the degree of hotness or coldness as measured on an arbitrary scale (eg in degrees Celsius). Plants have extreme variations of preferred temperature but this variable is of particular importance when

dealing with young growing plants, greenhouse plants, plants grown from seeds or cuttings and during PROPAGATION and fruiting periods.

tender adj

(of a plant) liable to be damaged by cold or frost when planted outside. Tender plants should be moved to a frost-free room or greenhouse if there is any danger of such conditions.

tender annual n

an ANNUAL that requires continued greenhouse cultivation.

tendril n

a slender spirally coiling sensitive organ that attaches a plant to its support. It allows plants such as sweet peas and grapes to climb.

tendril climber n

a plant that has tendrils and can thus climb on a support, eg sweet pea.

tepal n

the individual segment of a PERIANTH that cannot be clearly distinguished as a SEPAL or petal, eg in the flowers of the crocus and the tulip.

terete adj

(of a plant part) approximately cylindrical with a smooth surface. The term is usually used to describe a stem.

terminal adj

(of a plant part) referring to the uppermost leaf, branch, flower, bud or shoot at the end of extended plant growth.

ternate adj
1 *(of a plant or leaf)* composed of three subdivisions, eg of three leaflets. **2** (*of a leaf)* arranged in a group of three.

terrarium n
a closed container, usually made of glass or transparent plastic, in which plants are grown indoors.

terrestrial adj
(of a plant) referring to plants grown in soil as opposed to on rocks or in water.

tessellated adj
(of petals or leaves) having a distinct chequered pattern contrasting in either shade or colour with its background, eg some fritillaries.

tetraploid adj
(of a plant) containing twice the normal number of CHROMOSOMES. Such plants have four sets rather than two and often exhibit increased growth. Compare DIPLOID and TRIPLOID.

thermometer n
an instrument for determining temperature; usually a glass bulb attached to a fine graduated tube of glass and containing liquid mercury that rises and falls with changes of weather. It is of special importance in the greenhouse where temperature must be carefully monitored. Some models show maximum and minimum temperatures. Soil thermometers are also available.

thermostat n
an automatic device for regulating temperature,

used in the heating system of a propagator or greenhouse.

thin out vt

1 to reduce (the number of seedlings) in a bed or container so that others have more room to develop. Also called single. When the thinned seedlings are to be replanted, the term usually used is prick out. **2** to reduce (the number of flower or fruit buds) to prevent overcrowding and improve the quality of the fruit that does grow. **3** to reduce (the number of shoots and branches) on trees to prevent overcrowding.

thiram n

an inorganic fungicide with a wide range of uses. As a wettable powder it can control botrytis on tomatoes, lettuce etc. As a powder it may be dusted on seeds to protect them against soil-borne diseases. It is also useful for preventing the DAMPING-OFF of seedlings.

thorn n

see SPINE.

thrips n, pl **thrips**

a group of tiny insects that resemble the EARWIG. They are yellow to black and very narrow. They attack leaves, stems and flowers, causing distortion and silvery streaks, and can also prevent the opening of flower buds. Thrips can be controlled with insecticide or with SMOKES under glass. Also called THUNDERFLY.

thunderfly n

see THRIPS.

The branches indicated by
dotted lines are removed.
thinning out

[1]tie n

any material which fastens a plant to its support. Most ties are made of rustproof garden twine or plastic raffia. Sometimes soft metal is used.

[2]tie vt

to fasten (a plant) to its support.

till vt

to cultivate (the soil), eg to DIG, FORK, HOE or RAKE.

tilth n

the fine, crumbly surface layer of soil, usually provided by tilling.

tine n

a single prong of a CULTIVATOR, FORK or RAKE.

tip-bearing adj

(of a tree) applying to fruit trees which produce fruit buds on the tips of their shoots.

tip cutting n

a STEM CUTTING from the uppermost growth of a non-flowering plant shoot.

tip layering n

a method of layering used on plants, eg blackberries, that have shoots or stems which can be bent to the ground. The stem tips are buried in soil and kept moist until new roots are formed.

tomentose adj

(of a plant) covered with densely matted, usually short hairs.

top cutting n

see STEM CUTTING.

tip layering

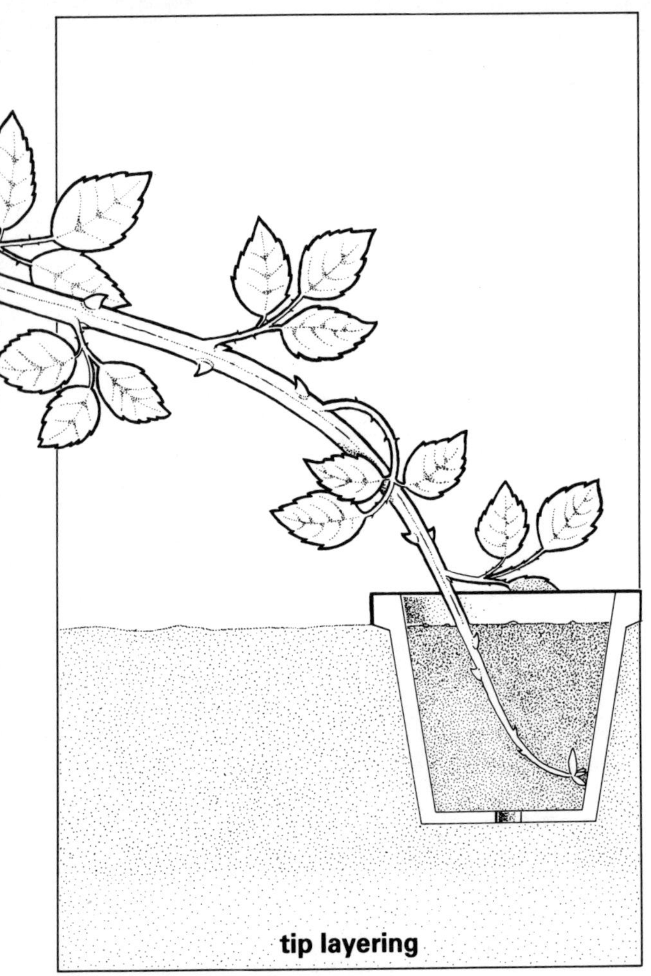

top dressing n
the application of a layer of compost, soil or fertilizer, usually to plants in pots or to established plants in a confined area. Some old soil should be removed from pots before top dressing is added. Top dressing of a lawn refers to an application of fertilizer to the lawn surface. See also MULCH. Compare BASE DRESSING.

top fruit n
edible fruit (eg apples, pears, plums, peaches) that grows on trees. Also known as TREE FRUIT. Compare SOFT FRUIT.

topiary n
the practice or art of training, cutting and trimming trees or shrubs into odd or ornamental shapes.

topsoil n
the top layer of the soil which under normal conditions is reasonably fertile. Compare SUBSOIL.

topworking n
a method of grafting similar to FRAMEWORKING in which an established tree is cut down to the trunk and the stubs of main branches and SCIONS are inserted to create new growth.

total weedkiller n
a weedkiller which destroys all vegetable matter that it touches, eg simazine or paraquat. Extremely poisonous, these chemicals must be used with great care.

trace element n
a chemical element important to the growth of a plant but needed only in minute quantities. These include BORON, IRON, and MANGANESE. Their absence may cause poor growth but an excess can be harmful. Many compound fertilizers contain them.

train vt
to manage (plants) in such a way as to make them grow in a certain direction or form. See also PRUNE, SUPPORT, TIE.

transpiration n
the normal escape of water into the air from the leaves of plants. Most water enters plants through their roots and goes out through their leaves. This is an essential part of PHOTOSYNTHESIS, but too much water loss can cause wilting and eventual death.

transplant vt
to move (a plant) from one place to another, usually to allow it more room to develop or to obtain a better environment. It is essential that such plants are firmly replanted and carefully watered.

transplanting spray n
see ANTI-TRANSPIRANT.

tread vt
to walk heavily on (recently cultivated soil) before preparing for sowing, planting or transplanting. This enables plant roots which develop subsequently to obtain close contact with

soil particles in order to take up nutrients and water.

tree n

a tall, woody PERENNIAL plant having a single usually long and erect main stem, generally with few or no branches on its lower part. Small trees and large shrubs are often confused.

tree fruit n

see TOP FRUIT.

[1]**trench** n

a length of soil dug to about three SPITS deep, usually provided for vegetable crops requiring BLANCHING or for ANNUAL crops which benefit from applications of organic matter in the trench.

[2]**trench** vt

to dig (the soil) to a depth of three spits. Compare DOUBLE DIG, SINGLE DIG.

trickle irrigation n

a means of delivering moisture to individual plants in which a flexible tube is perforated or fitted with nozzles at various intervals. Sometimes small tubes are fed from a larger one. This method is especially useful for watering plants under glass.

trifoliate adj

(of a leaf) having three leaflets.

trimmer n

a tool, powered either by an electric motor or a petrol engine, that is used for cutting relatively light vegetation and small areas of grass (eg lawn edges and steep banks) inaccessible to a mower. The cutter is usually a nylon line wound on a spool; larger models, often known as brushcutters, may also be fitted with metal or plastic blades and can cut tougher vegetation (eg brambles).

tripartite adj

(of a plant part) cut into three lobes. The term usually refers to bracts, petals, leaves or sepals.

triple cordon n

see CORDON.

triploid adj

(of a plant) containing three sets of CHROMOSOMES.This often occurs when plants with normal sets of chromosomes are crossed with those with twice the number. The resulting plant is often sterile. Compare DIPLOID and TETRAPLOID.

tropical adj

(of a plant) originating in the tropics. These plants need to be grown in warm conditions, indoors or in a greenhouse, with a minimum temperature of 18°C (64°F).

tropical house n

a warm, humid greenhouse with a temperature of about 21°C (70°F).

trowel n

a garden tool with a short handle, usually used for setting out small plants or bulbs. The blade is typically narrow, but may be broad or graduated.

true-breeding adj

(of a plant) having flowers that, when fertilized with their own pollen, form seeds which produce seedlings nearly identical to the parent plant. Compare HYBRID.

trug n
a shallow, long basket, made of wood or plastic, used for carrying small plants, garden tools, vegetables and flowers.

[1]**trumpet** adj
(of a flower) having a flared opening shaped like a trumpet. In such plants the COROLLA is at least as long as the CALYX, eg as in most daffodils.

[2]**trumpet** n
a flower or part of a flower which is trumpet-shaped.

[1]**truncate** vt
to shorten (a plant part) by cutting off a part.

[2]**truncate** adj
(of a leaf) having the end square or even.

trunk n
the main stem of a tree, as distinguished from branches and roots.

truss n
a compact cluster of fruits or flowers at the end of a stem.

tuber n
a thickened or swollen underground root or stem that stores food and is potentially able to produce a new plant, eg a potato.

tubercle n
a small knobby swelling or a small tuber, eg the nodules on LEGUMINOUS plants and on cacti.

tubular floret n
one of the FLORETS typical of many flowers in the family *Compositae,* usually packed in the centre to form the inner disc. Some flowers of this

family are composed of tubular florets only, eg the cornflower. Compare RAY FLORET.

tufa n

a porous rock formed as a deposit by springs; a type of limestone. Its ability to absorb and retain moisture makes it very useful in a rock garden.

tunic n

the enclosing or covering membrane or tissue of a seed, bulb or corm. A tunic can be fibrous, papery or thick and coarse.

[1]**turf** n, pl **turves**

1 a piece of the upper layer of soil bound by grass and plant roots into a thick mat. **2** a piece of dried PEAT. **3** a stretch of grass. See also LAWN.

[2]**turf** vt

to cover with turf; to make a lawn. It is a quicker method of creating a lawn than to sow seed.

turfing iron n

a tool with a heart-shaped blade used for undercutting and lifting turves after the sides have been cut.

turgid adj

(of a plant) full of water, the natural condition of a healthy plant. A plant that is not turgid will wilt.

turion n

1 a shoot grown in winter from a bud on an underground RHIZOME. It forms a shoot above ground in summer. **2** the resting winter shoot of some aquatic plants. These either float or rest on a pond's bottom and form new plants in the spring or summer.

2,4-D n

a powerful selective weedkiller that kills broadleaved plants but not grass.

2,4,5-T n

a powerful SYSTEMIC weedkiller used to control shrubs or woody weeds, eg brambles and nettles. Owing to evidence that it may contain a carcinogenic impurity, it has been banned in several countries and has been voluntarily withdrawn from sale to gardeners in Britain.

type n

the individual plant of any species that was first described botanically and thus accepted for CLASSIFICATION. Any deviation from the type is given a VARIETY name, even if it is more common than the originally classified type.

umbel n
an INFLORESCENCE typical of plants of the carrot family in which the axis is very much more contracted so that the flower stalks spring from the same point to form a flat or rounded flower cluster.

underplant vt
to grow (small plants) among or under taller plants.

undulate adj
(of a leaf or petal) having a wavy surface, edge or margins.

unisexual adj
(of a flower) being of one sex; having only female PISTILS or male STAMENS.

urea n
a NITROGEN-containing compound that is present in urine and is a final product of protein decomposition. Synthesized as a fertilizer, it is quick acting and can be applied directly or dissolved in water.

variegated adj
(of a leaf or flower) being speckled or spotted with contrasting colours; dappled.

variety n
1 a variation of a SPECIES that is distinct and thus given a name of its own. **2** a group of plants within a species which has constant characteristics separating it from the typical form and from other varieties within the species. See classification.

vegetable n
a herbaceous plant (eg cabbage, bean or potato) grown for an edible part (leaves, seeds, roots, tubers etc) which is usually eaten with the main course of a meal rather than as a dessert. Botanically speaking, such vegetables as tomatoes and marrows are actually fruits.

vegetative adj
(of a plant) being capable of growth. In this sense all plant parts except flowers are vegetative.

vegetative propagation n
the increase of plants by non-sexual processes or methods. Artificial methods include CUTTINGS, GRAFTING, DIVISION or LAYERING. Natural means of vegetative propagation include the

production of RUNNERS and OFFSETS.

ventilation n

the process of providing air movement. Ventilation is necessary in greenhouses when the temperature is too high or the atmosphere too moist. It is usually provided by opening windows but an electrically controlled system of ventilation is available.

vermiculite n

any of various minerals of hydrous silicates derived from mica that expand on heating to form a lightweight, highly water-absorbent, sterile material. These qualities make it ideal for sowing seeds and rooting cuttings, but once established plants should be transplanted, as vermiculite contains few nutrients.

vernalization n

the act of hastening the flowering and fruiting of plants, especially by chilling seeds, bulbs or seedlings. This process brings on the reproductive phase more quickly. Compare STRATIFICATION.

verticillium wilt n

a fungal disease affecting a wide range of herbaceous plants and some shrubs and trees. It causes infected plants to develop brown patches on their stems and to wilt.

vigour n

(the capacity for) active, healthy, well-balanced growth in a plant. See also HYBRID VIGOUR.

virus disease n

a term covering a large variety of plant diseases. Organisms causing virus may be smaller than bacteria and fungi, and are often too small to be detected with a microscope. They cause a range of symptoms which weaken plants, from mottled or dry foliage to overall stunting. The most common means by which virus disease is transmitted is by sap-sucking insects, but birds, tools and humans can also be the agents. There is no real cure for infected plants, which should be destroyed.

viviparous adj

1 *(of a plant)* germinating while still attached to the parent plant. A few plants' seeds germinate in this way and the term also refers to plants that produce smaller plants or bulblets on the stem or leaf, eg many lilies. **2** *(of an animal)* producing living young instead of eggs. The APHID is the only garden pest of this sort.

wasp n
any of numerous largely flesh-eating slender narrow-waisted insects, many of which have an extremely painful sting, especially a very common social wasp with black and yellow stripes. Wasps eat ripe fruit, which may be protected with bags, but can be beneficial by destroying more harmful pests. They may be destroyed with their nest, preferably after dark.

water n
the colourless, odourless liquid which descends from the clouds. It is one of the ingredients vital to plant life and plants grown in containers must be frequently supplied with it. Rainwater is considered most suitable for plants; tapwater must sometimes be used with care, since if it comes from a chalky area it may be harmful to lime-hating plants.

water garden n
a (section of a) garden containing a pond or stream, and often with additional features such as a fountain or artificial waterfall, that is devoted to aquatic plants, marsh plants, ornamental fish, etc.

watering can n
a vessel with a handle and a long spout, usually fitted with a ROSE (a fitting with many small holes), used for watering plants. Available in metal or plastic and in capacities from one pint to two gallons, watering cans can be fitted with various attachments, eg spray applicators.

water shoot n
a long, quick-growing growth on a fruit tree arising from a bud growing on a branch. Such shoots can cause overcrowding and are unfruitful and should be removed by cutting off at the base.

[1]**weed** n
an unwanted plant which often overgrows or chokes out more desirable plants. The term is usually applied to a wild plant, but a cultivated plant that becomes over-profuse or invasive is effectively a weed. It can be destroyed by pulling, chopping or applying weedkiller.

[2]**weed** vt
to clear (land) of weeds.

weedkiller n
any chemical material that destroys weeds, sometimes referred to as a HERBICIDE. It is categorized according to action as CONTACT, SELECTIVE or SYSTEMIC, or designated a TOTAL WEEDKILLER.

weeping adj
(of a tree or shrub) having slender drooping branches; of pendulous habit.

weevil n
any of numerous usually small beetles,

characterized by a long snout bearing jaws at the tip, many of which are injurious, especially in the larval stage, to grain, fruit and foliage. These include the vine, apple blossom and pea and bean weevils. Others attack nuts, vegetables, berries, root plants and cotton. Weevils can be controlled with insecticide, although some are heavily resistant.

wheelbarrow n

a load-carrying device consisting of a shallow box supported at one end by a single wheel and at the other by a stand (when at rest) or by handles (when being pushed).

whip n

an unbranched, young shoot of a woody plant, often the first year's growth from a graft or bud.

whip and tongue graft n

a type of graft usually used on young trees in which ROOTSTOCK and SCION of similar thickness are cut so as to interlock before being bound and sealed.

whip graft n

see SPLICE GRAFT.

whitefly n

any of numerous small white insects that are injurious plant pests related to the SCALE INSECT. It is not a real fly and is particularly destructive to plants under glass. Tomatoes and brassicas are most often damaged. Both adult insects and the young they produce suck sap from plants. Some pesticides may be effective and greenhouse FUMIGATION is also helpful; but perhaps the best solution, in appropriate circumstances, is biological control.

whorl n

an arrangement of similar anatomical parts (eg leaves) in a circle around a point on an axis (eg a stem). Such leaves or flowers usually arise from one point in a pattern resembling the spokes of a wheel. Also known as circle.

whorled adj

(of a leaf arrangement) having three or more leaves growing in a circle from one stem node.

widger n

a small, long and narrow hand-held garden tool, resembling a shoehorn. It is used to prick out seedlings.

wild adj

(of a plant) growing without the aid and care of humans; not cultivated. Many so-called wild plants (eg cowslips and common toadflax) are, in fact, now quite commonly cultivated as part of a trend of increasing interest in wild flowers and ecology.

wildlife garden n

a garden devoted to growing wild native plants and providing a refuge for wild animals in areas similar to their natural habitats. Paradoxically, many wildlife gardens need careful establishment and maintenance; they should not merely be an excuse for letting one's garden be overrun by weeds.

[1]**wilt** vi

to flag or droop. Wilting in plants is generally

caused by pest damage, lack of moisture, excessively high temperatures, external damage, fungus attack or damage to the roots.

[2]wilt n

any of numerous diseases which cause plants to droop and collapse. Many are soil-borne and destroy roots and stems. Most of these diseases can be carried by fungi or bacteria; others are caused by virus attack. Typically the condition is incurable and the affected plant must be destroyed.

window box n

a trough, usually made of timber or plastic, designed to hold soil for growing plants and to be placed on a windowsill or be suspended from it.

windbreak n

a growth of trees or a hedge or fence that breaks the force of the wind. Exposed gardens and those near the coast or in high flat areas especially need protection from the wind.

wing n

1 a leaf-like or membranous rigid appendage found on many fruits, on the leafstalks of citrus and on some seeds. **2** the side petal found on a sweet pea flower.

winter garden n

a garden devoted to plants which flourish in winter, eg by flowering or retaining attractive foliage.

winter killing n

the killing of twigs not hardy enough to survive winter months. Winter-killed twigs should be pruned at the time when the old wood of shrubs and trees is putting out new shoots in the spring.

winter moth n

a moth which lays eggs on fruit trees, especially apple, in the winter. Its caterpillars hatch out in the spring and quickly eat all the new foliage if not controlled by insecticide. WINTER-WASH can kill the eggs before the caterpillars hatch.

winter pruning n

the cutting back of deciduous trees (especially fruit trees) in the dormant season, usually from November onwards. New trees require harder pruning to encourage growth; older trees require less, only enough to improve the shape of the tree.

winter-wash n

an insecticide or fungicide applied during winter months, especially a TAR OIL WASH or other chemicals sprayed on fruit trees to control insects and their eggs.

wireworm n

the slender hard-coated LARVA of any of various beetles, especially destructive to plant roots, tubers and bulbs. Cultivation of soil reduces the population because it exposes them to birds. Some pesticide dusts may also be applied.

witches' broom n

an abnormal, bushy growth caused by a parasitic fungus. It is often found on blueberries, but more usually on woody cedars and other woody plants. It can sap the tree's vigour, but is easily cut out.

wood ash n
a fertilizer which results from burning wood and other vegetable matter. It provides a valuable source of POTASH, as well as small amounts of other nutrients. Wood ash from young growth is higher in potash content. It must be worked into the soil; otherwise it can form a surface layer and even destroy soil texture.

wood bud n
a bud which grows into a shoot, as opposed to developing into a flower.

woodlouse n
a small ground-living crustacean with a flattened elliptical body, often capable of rolling into a ball in defence. It prefers dark, moist, rotting conditions and often destroys roots and stems near the soil, especially those of young plants. Slug pellets, traps or pesticides are forms of control.

woody adj
(of a plant part) tough, fibrous, and not soft.

worm n
the soil-living creature commonly called an earthworm. It is of use in the cultivated garden because of its ability to aerate soil and to speed up the production of HUMUS, but it can cause serious damage to pot plants if it enters the soil in a container.

xerophytic adj
(of a plant) structurally adapted for life and growth with a limited water supply, either by the storage of moisture in the tissue of the leaf or stem or by the reduction of leaves and stems; eg cacti, gorse and heather.

zinc n
a naturally occurring metallic element which is a TRACE ELEMENT essential for plant growth.

zineb n
an inorganic fungicide that is effective against leaf diseases, RUST, MILDEW and potato BLIGHT. It is available as a wettable powder or dust. Although generally safe it can cause irritation of the skin and eyes.

zygomorphic, zygomorphous adj
(of a flower) capable of being divided into two similar halves in one plane only, eg snapdragon, orchid and foxglove. Compare ACTINOMORPHIC.

Pronunciation of plant names

Botanical names of plants are pronounced in a variety of ways by different people. This is not wholly surprising, since most of them are hybrid words consisting of a Latin ending tagged onto the name of a person or a word from another language. It is frequently impossible to guess the common English pronunciation from the spelling; and a knowledge of classical Latin is more often a distraction than a help. The following list gives the most usual pronunciations of a hundred awkward genus names, although it cannot possibly include all the variants that one hears. The sounds are represented as follows:

Vowels

a	as in	b*a*d, f*a*t
ah	,,	f*a*ther, oomp*ah*
aw	,,	s*aw*, *aw*ful
ay	,,	m*a*ke, h*ay*
e	,,	b*e*d, h*ea*d
ee	,,	sh*ee*p, k*ey*
eə	,,	th*ere*, h*air*
i	,,	sh*i*p, man*y*
ie	,,	b*i*te, l*ie*d
iə	,,	h*ere*, f*ear*
o	,,	p*o*t, cr*o*p
oh	,,	n*o*te, J*oa*n
oo	,,	p*u*t, c*oo*k
ooh	,,	b*oo*t, l*u*te
ow	,,	n*ow*, b*ough*
oy	,,	b*oy*, l*oi*ter
u	,,	c*u*t, l*u*ck
uh	,,	b*i*rd, abs*u*rd
ə	,,	moth*er*, *a*bout

Consonants

ch	as in	*ch*eer
g	,,	*g*ay
h	,,	*h*ot
j	,,	*j*ump
ng	,,	su*ng*
s	,,	*s*oon
sh	,,	fi*sh*
th	,,	*th*ing
y	,,	*y*et
z	,,	*z*ero

b, d, f, k, l, m, n, p, r, t, v, w have their usual English sound-values

A dot is used to separate syllables. The syllable in **bold** type is the one on which the main accent falls.

abies	**ay**·bi·eez *or* **a**·bi·eez
acacia	ə·**kay**·shə *or* ə·**kay**·syə
acaena	ə·**see**·nə
acer	**ay**·sə
agave	ə·**gah**·vi
ailanthus	ay·**lan**·thəs *or* ie·**lan**·thəs
alstroemeria	al·strə·**miə**·ri·ə
amelanchier	am·ə·**lang**·ki·ə *or* am·ə·**lan**·shi·ə
anchusa	an·**chooh**·sə
antirrhinum	an·ti·**rie**·nəm
araucaria	a·raw·**keə**·ri·ə
aubrietia	aw·**bree**·shə
ancuba	**aw**·kyew·bə
azalea	ə·**zay**·li·ə
bergenia	buh·**gee**·ni·ə
billbergia	bil·**buh**·gi·ə *or* bil·**buh**·ji·ə
bougainvillea	booh·gən·**vil**·i·ə
buddleia	**bud**·li·ə
calceolaria	kal·si·ə·**leə**·ri·ə
camellia	kə·**mee**·li·ə *or (less frequent)* kə·**me**·li·ə
catalpa	kə·**tal**·pə
catananche	kat·ə·**nang**·ki
ceanothus	see·ə·**noh**·thəs
chaenomeles	kee·noh·**mee**·leez
chamaecyparis	ka·mi·**si**·pə·rəs
cheiranthus	kie·**ran**·thəs
chimonanthus	kie·moh·**nan**·thəs
chionodoxa	kie·ə·noh·**dok**·sə *or* kie·on·ə·**dok**·sə
choisya	**shwah**·zi·ə *or* **choy**·zi·ə
cineraria	si·nə·**reə**·ri·ə
cotoneaster	kə·toh·ni·**as**·tə
crataegus	krə·**tee**·gəs
cyclamen	**sik**·lə·mən
cytisus	**si**·tis·əs

decaisnea	də·**kay**·ni·ə
deutzia	**dyooht**·si·ə *or* **doyt**·si·ə
dicentra	die·**sen**·trə
dieffenbachia	dee·fən·**bak**·i·ə
dracaena	drə·**see**·nə
elaeagnus	el·ee·**ag**·nəs
erigeron	i·**rij**·ə·ron *or* i·**rig**·ə·ron
eschscholtzia	e·**sholt**·si·ə *or* i·**skol**·shə *or* es·**kolt**·si·ə
euonymus	yooh·**on**·i·məs
ficus	**fie**·kəs
fuchsia	**fyooh**·shə
gaillardia	gay·**lah**·di·ə
gaultheria	gawl·**thiə**·ri·ə
geum	**jee**·əm
gingko *or* ginkgo	**gingk**·goh *or* **ging**·koh
godetia	goh·**dee**·shə
gypsophila	jip·**sof**·i·lə
hedera	**hed**·ə·rə
hebe	**hee**·bi
hemerocallis	hem·ə·roh·**kal**·is
heuchera	**hoy**·kə·rə *or* **hyooh**·kə·rə
hibiscus	hi·**bis**·kəs *or* hie·**bis**·kəs
howeia	**how**·i·ə
hypoestes	hie·poh·**es**·teez
ipomoea	i·poh·**mi**·ə *or* ie·poh·**mi**·ə *or* ie·**poh**·mi·ə
kalanchoe	kal·ən·**koh**·i
kniphofia	nip·**hoh**·fi·ə *or (less frequent)* nie·**foh**·fi·ə
koelreuteria	kuhl·roy·**tiə**·ri·ə
kolkwitzia	kohl·**kwit**·si·ə
leycesteria	les·**tiə**·ri·ə
lobelia	loh·**bee**·li·ə
mahonia	mə·**hoh**·ni·ə

maranta	mə·**ran**·tə
meconopsis	me·kə·**nop**·sis
mesembryanthemum	mi·zem·bri·**an**·thi·məm
myosotis	mie·oh·**soh**·tis
nemesia	nə·**mee**·zi·ə
nicotiana	ni·**koh**·shi·ah·nə *or* ni·**koh**·shi·ay·nə
nigella	nie·**jel**·ə
oenothera	ee·noh·**thiə**·rə *or* ee·**noth**·ə·rə
olearia	oh·li·**eə**·ri·ə
opuntia	o·**pun**·shi·ə *or* oh·**pun**·shi·ə
paulownia	paw·**loh**·ni·ə *or (less frequent)* paw·**lov**·ni·ə
penstemon	pen·**stee**·mən
physalis	**fie**·sə·lis *or* fie·**say**·lis
physostegia	fie·soh·**stee**·ji·ə
pieris	**pie**·ə·ris *or (less frequent)* piə·ris
poinsettia	poyn·**set**·i·ə
ranunculus	rə·**nung**·kyoo·ləs
ribes	**rie**·beez
saintpaulia	saynt·**paw**·li·ə
sansevieria	san·si·**viə**·ri·ə
schizanthus	ski·**zan**·thəs *or* skit·**san**·thəs
sedum	**see**·dəm
selaginella	se·**la**·jə·nel·ə
sequoia	si·**kwoy**·ə
sidalcea	sie·**dal**·shi·ə
solanum	soh·**lay**·nəm
spiraea	spie·**ri**·ə
tagetes	ta·**jee**·teez *or* **taj**·i·teez
tradescantia	tra·dəs·**kan**·shi·ə
tropaeolum	troh·**pee**·ə·ləm
tsuga	t·**sooh**·gə *or* **sooh**·gə
weigela	wie·**jee**·lə *or* wie·**gee**·lə *or* wie·**jel**·ə
wisteria *or* wistaria	wis·**tiə**·ri·ə *or* wis·**teə**·ri·ə
yucca	**yuk**·ə